THE ASTRONAUT,
THE CAKE, AND TOMORROW

Published under licence 2012 by Searching Finance Ltd.

ISBN: 978-1-907720-75-8

Typeset and designed by Deirdré Gyenes

THE ASTRONAUT, THE CAKE, AND TOMORROW

Written by
Matt Sisson

Illustrations by
Matthew James Kay

Searching
finance

About the author

Matt Sisson is a campaigner, blogger and a local coordinator for the Green Party.

About Searching Finance

Searching Finance Ltd is a dynamic new voice in knowledge provision for the financial services and related professional sectors. For more information, please visit www.searchingfinance.com.

CONTENTS

PREFACE AND ACKNOWLEDGEMENTS

THIS IS A BOOK about how humanity can transform its economic and financial systems to overcome the challenges posed by climate breakdown, and to live within the sustainable capacity of the Earth. The current configuration of human development, with our expansive economic systems at the centre, has a devastating impact on the Earth and threatens the existence of global civilisation as we know it.

Economics holds a significant position in our understanding of the world, and our developed societies seem especially formulated to submit to the interests of money and the power it wields. As a result, it's hard to maintain hope that solutions might emerge. Yet I've found that the more the perceived wisdoms of economics are challenged, the easier sustainable alternatives become clear. We find it so hard to see a different future because we're regularly fed assumptions about our economy, our financial systems, and human nature that obfuscate the bigger picture. In almost every case, I believe the solutions are clearer, simpler, and more intuitive than the problems they succeed. This is empowering and means that an economics degree is not required to join in the debate. Economics loves its confusing jargon, but most concepts are simpler than they may first appear.

It is also important to state that this book does not irrefutably evidence the existence of climate change, or the many other disruptive and destructive impacts of humanity on the Earth's essential systems. If you have read widely but are still able to disregard the overwhelming consensus evidence as congregated in places like the United Nation's Intergovernmental Panel on Climate Change (IPCC) reports, or any of the countless books written by leading environmental scientists, then it is unlikely you will find anything here to convince you otherwise. There comes a point in any debate where we no longer need to start the argument from first principles. I therefore start with the assumption that as the massive body of evidence, assembled by countless thousands of experts all over the globe, concludes with overwhelming consensus that climate change is real, man-made, and dangerous, that this point has been reached. If you are looking to discover more about climate breakdown then there are many other books that marshal the evidence far more completely than this one. It is my hope that the environmental sections in this book are enough to provide a whistle-stop tour of the realities we face, in order to set in context the economic changes that are discussed later.

Whilst this book has a global scope in places, it is written with a focus on the United Kingdom. This is because I hope that it will contribute to changes in the way that society, politics, and the economy works in my own country. That doesn't mean that the arguments do not equally apply elsewhere; one of the features of our economic and financial systems is that they are almost universally replicated across the globe. In addition, many of the solutions listed in this book can, with little alteration or extra imagination, be enacted in any country individually and at any time, without need to wait for a global agreement. There may be international implications for a country taking lone action, and it may also be that some ideas would prove more effective if enacted by many countries at once. This is certainly true of efforts to combat climate change in general. That being said, I believe the merits of applying these solutions mean they are worth implementing nationally and as soon as possible.

Finally, I believe that the ideas portrayed in this book work together to form a cohesive, if controversial, whole. Taken together they provide a framework within which human civilisation may be able to exist sustainably, within the boundaries of our finite planet. I claim little originality; I am grateful for all of those who have put their creative energies into the research and critique that this book draws upon, and is inspired by. Whilst the vision of the future promoted in the following chapters is one that will hopefully appeal to many, there are some who will not agree with it. That's fine of course; it's the mark of a healthy civil society that people can be critical and have different opinions. However, it's important that if people disagree with something they don't just criticise, but wrestle with the challenges that we face and put forward legitimate and considered alternatives. The stakes are too high to leave this to someone else.

***

Now to a few notes of thanks. It is apparent that I wouldn't have ever started on the project, or even thought it was possible, without the enthusiasm of Ashwin Rattan of Searching Finance for what were, at best, embryonic ideas. I am grateful for our chance meeting, and the opportunity he has given me to develop and publish my work.

I'm also very thankful for the support of my wife Rachael. As well as her constant encouragement throughout the process, over the last eight years she has played a formative role in helping me become someone who can finish things, rather than just start them. Her work is not yet done.

I'm grateful for the friendship and input of Dr Tom Kane and Dr Matt Pain. Our regular lunchtime discussions have been the primary sounding-board for my ideas, and they have both been kind and diplomatic in spending many hours reviewing my drafts, offering feedback, and pointing out the weaknesses in the texts. Chris Hardisty has been a great encouragement and has provided invaluable feedback on earlier drafts of the book. My sister Jaya has reviewed much of the text from a younger perspective, and the book is stronger for her views on the areas that weren't as accessible as I'd initially hoped.

Finally, I wish to thank Matthew Kay, whose brilliant illustrations both capture and enhance the character of the book, and give it a heart that I do not think would be apparent with the words alone. His friendship, insight, and regular picture updates have been supportive to the extent that I see the book as something of a joint project.

MATT SISSON

INTRODUCTION

THE UNITED KINGDOM is a great country. It is extremely wealthy, ranked in the top twenty for the amount of wealth averaged across the population (known as GDP per capita). In 2013 the UK was listed third in a global opinion poll of how positively countries are regarded, behind only Germany and Canada . Yet it doesn't really feel like Britain is a great country at the moment. Like anyone else, we Britons want to be excited about life and about the future. We want to be happy. Instead many of us often feel anxious about the future as well as the present. We feel detached from our local communities and the people around us, if we even know who they are. We want this to change, but we're not sure what to do about it. We're told there is no alternative. We feel helpless and apathetic. What's more, this experience appears to be reflected in other countries too. A quick glance at news websites across any given week demonstrates that as a global civilisation we face the wider challenges of vast inequality, widespread impoverishment caused by breakdowns in financial and economic systems, and environmental issues that we seem incapable of addressing.

But what if it could be different? What if we could be excited about the future again? What if we could imagine a better future for ourselves and our children in a safer, friendlier, happier, and more prosperous country? It is certainly possible to make big changes to the way our society, our government, and our economy operate, and it can happen in our lifetime.

We should be allowed to get excited about, and look forward to, the future and not have to wake up every morning to bad economic news and talk of 'a lost generation'.

Often when new ideas are suggested about how to make the country better, the response is 'that's good, but it will never happen'. This kind of view is commonly held and it's not surprising. It's very easy to accept the country as it is today, as if it's always been like this. However, the reality is that our country and the world around it are constantly changing, and if we went back in time even just thirty or forty years then our society and culture would probably seem very alien to us. Things are the way they are because of decisions made by people, and if people made those decisions, then people can change them again. Human history is littered with stories of people and peoples who, against the odds, succeeded in changing their communities and countries for the better. If enough people decide they want something enough, then history shows they can make it happen.

How do we know what we want to change, and change to what? A few vague ideas about what we think might be wrong doesn't make a manifesto, or a movement. A good way to think about what we would like to change is to imagine what we would want the country to look like and be like in the future, in ten or twenty years' time for example. It's important to be able to do this because if we can't imagine a different future then we are less likely to create one that we're happy with. Alternatively, if we know where we want to go then we can plan for it, and have a whole lot more fun getting there.

One problem with our political leadership is that they don't seem to have a very clear idea of what they want the future to look like, or if they do, they're not very good at communicating it. Most of the time they make policies and plans that seem to be based on wanting to stay in power or get re-elected rather than planning for the long term. The current government are currently enforcing policies of 'austerity' that in practice mean trying to save money by reducing government spending in the short term, whilst appearing to ignore the long-term social and economic consequences. Sometimes problems need quick fixes, but most of the time what we need instead is good, consistent, long-term planning that envisions a hopeful, prosperous future for Britain and generations of Britons to come, and then carefully but assuredly brings that into being.

So this book is about politics; yet at the same time it is about more than that phrase would suggest. It's about life and how we live. It's about our relationship with the Earth and each other, and the way that our presence in this universe is not just about our existence but our experience. In short, it's about big ideas. However, just because things are big, this doesn't mean they have to be complicated. Most ideas, however big, can be explained in simple ways, and that's what this book tries to do. Big ideas are important because whether we realise it or not, the big ideas frame all the little ones.

Unfortunately, our politicians don't often talk about the ideas that underpin the policies that they make, and when they do, it can be hard to follow the connection between the two. Often they seem much more content to debate individual policies in great detail. As an example, politicians often talk about, and debate, taxes. They might want to introduce a new tax, or take one away, or make an existing one bigger or smaller; sometimes who 'wins' and who 'loses out' from tax changes seems to be chosen almost arbitrarily. One year pensioners might get a bit more money, the next year they might get less. One year Value Added Tax (VAT) might go up by a bit whilst taxes on higher earners go down, only for changes to be reversed soon after. In many cases the decisions seem largely inconsequential; in some they seem irrational. Very occasionally they sort-of make sense. Most of the time the explanations given are complicated, or we simply don't know enough about them to understand what implications they have. Programmes on the TV or radio will be broadcast where a 'balanced' range of opinions from all sorts of different experts are offered, but these experts in most cases, simply talk about the impact the changes will have on them or their own interests.

Where we can understand the implications, few government policies actually seem to form part of a cohesive whole. This is because the values or ideas behind them either don't exist, or aren't made clear. Instead we see political clashes and point-scoring over the fine details of policies that will have little impact on how our society or economy fundamentally operate. In these instances, it really can seem like our politicians are the only people in the country that can't see that something's wrong; that can't see the iceberg. They are the cabin crew rearranging the deckchairs on the Titanic.

This apparent lack of imagination and action from our politicians is, both directly and indirectly, the result of a particularly extreme type of capitalist ideology known as 'neoliberalism', which has come to dominate the political and economic arenas of Western societies over the last thirty years. Among the British political parties the current Conservative Party holds most closely to neoliberal views, but large chunks of neoliberal theory are accepted by all three of the major parliamentary parties (the Conservatives, Labour, and the Liberal Democrats), as well as the UK Independence Party (UKIP). Neoliberalism says that most of the time governments just get in the way and make things worse, and that actually we'd all be better off if we left people and companies to interact free from the rules and regulations imposed by government. It says that people and companies should engage through this magical thing called the 'free market' (the main neoliberal buzzword), and be able to exchange their goods, services and labour for money, at a value that the free market decides. The term 'free market' implies by its name that it is free from control, and we associate the word 'free' with warm, positive feelings.

However, as we will explore later on in this book, the idea that there is, or could ever be, a way of interacting in a market that is free from government interference is flawed. You can only have and own things to exchange when you have a government to decide on, and enforce, property rights, or otherwise collectively submit to some form of rule that governs transactions within society. In addition companies only exist because governments establish a legal structure in a country, including all the laws that enable companies to be created and to have a separate legal identity from the humans that own or manage them. These rules often create other benefits such as limited liability, which means that if a business goes bust the business' owner won't have to go bankrupt with it. Even people who say they strongly believe in the idea of the 'free market' happily accept lots of government laws and regulations on trade without even thinking about it. How many people really want to see the return of slave or child labour, or think that police officers or soldiers should be for sale to the highest bidder?

Rules and regulations are everywhere. They provide the foundations of our society, and they provide us with a structure and limits within which we can thrive. They also demonstrate our values: the things that we think are important, and how we want to live as individuals and as a nation. Ha-Joon Chang, an economist at the University of Cambridge points out that we tend to ignore or not even notice the regulations that we like, and only notice the ones that we disagree with. So when someone says that they think we should have a free market, they're not talking about some magical system, they're saying that they value some things and not others, and that because of that there are some rules that they like, and some that they don't.

In addition, what our politicians often neglect to say is that within any system there are winners and there are losers, and that those with power (the 'winners') are most likely to change the system for their benefit, or maintain the status quo, where they are on top. When these injustices are discovered, as they frequently are, they only show more clearly the role that people play in shaping the systems in which we live. The world we live in might not have been cohesively designed from the top-down, but it certainly wasn't an accident. It is the end product of lots of decisions made by lots of people in powerful positions throughout time. Yet if people have made decisions then people can change them again, or make new ones. Once we recognise this it's easier to be hopeful about the possibilities for the future.

There are no magical ideas that we must adhere to at all costs; what there are instead are choices and policies, made by people, for people. They all have certain values behind them, and these values demonstrate who we are and what we believe about ourselves and each other. By acknowledging this, we can begin to think about what we like and don't like about our country, our economy and our society, and what we'd like to be different. Over the following chapters we'll explore some of these values, and look at what they lead to. This will give us a better idea of which ones we need to hold on to and which ones to let go of, in order to ensure a bright future that we can thoughtfully and deliberately plan into being, rather than a chaotic, difficult one that we stumble into by accident.

One last point before we continue: proponents of neoliberalism can sometimes seem to possess an Orwellian fear of 'grand visions' of anything; perhaps missing the fact that neoliberalism is itself such a grand vision. They fear a slippery slope to some kind of grim fascist or communist dystopia where inspiring ideology inevitably leads to disappointment and oppression; that somehow all collective endeavours are doomed to fail at best, and at worst lead ultimately to state-led villainy. This is not true. There's no rule that says that by putting lots of good ideas together at the same time into a cohesive whole they lead to something monstrous.

Similarly, some people possess a view that 'one person's utopia is another's dystopia'; that there's no point in searching for a better world, because everyone has a different idea of what that world might look like. This has elements of truth. There is no doubt that different people do have different ideas of what their 'ideal world' might consist of. However, this view ignores the fact that whilst the finer points may be in dispute, the majority of people can agree that there are many things that are just and unjust, or 'good' and 'bad', and could agree on what these might be. This is important, because the truth is that the challenges the human race faces during the 21st Century cannot, and will not, be solved except by collective action. These challenges cannot be faced by isolation and selfishness, but only by humanity coming together at local, national, and international levels around a set of principles and ideas that first enable us to dig ourselves out of the mess we've got into, and then provide the framework with which to move into an abundant, peaceful and sustainable future.

So what are these challenges? Let's start by looking at the one that underpins everything else; our impact on the planet that sustains us.

THE ASTRONAUT

In 1966 the Economist Kenneth E. Boulding wrote an essay called *The Economics of the Coming Spaceship Earth.*[9] The essay described how humans have tended to think about the world as if we were cowboys. Boulding argued that we needed to start thinking differently about the Earth, as well as human societies and economies, if we were to continue enjoying lives of prosperity for many years to come.

What he meant by this was that to previous generations - who didn't have modern technology like cars, phones, satellites, or advanced weaponry, or our knowledge of the world's geography - the Earth has always seemed huge, unknown and scary, much like the Wild West. For prior generations the Earth was a vast expanse of desert and mountains, forests, lakes, and seas that were too big to comprehend. For the cowboys and other adventurers, this huge land was there to be explored, and to be measured, tamed and controlled. The people living amongst this wilderness really were at the mercy of the land, the weather and the seasons; struggling to carve out a meagre, survivalist existence. They would have been keenly aware of the Earth's impact on them; an Earth of which they had very little understanding. However, their struggle with insignificance against the might of nature would have made it extremely difficult to conceive the impact they could possibly have on the Earth itself.

What Boulding recognised was that times have changed and that the ingenuity of humanity has now overcome most of the challenges and threats of nature. The development of agriculture has helped us to meet our nutritional needs and enabled us to stay in one place rather than living as nomads, following the herds. Our building technology has enabled us to create strong shelters and bustling settlements, giving us protection from the elements and allowing us to live close enough together to take advantage of our shared skills and resources. Our advances in navigation, transport, and mapping have 'shrunk' the Earth and opened up spaces and resources that were previously inaccessible for use and exploitation. Huge advances in sanitation, medicine, and healthcare have helped us overcome many previously debilitating and life-threatening ailments, and enabled the human population to grow at an incredible rate. In 2012 the human population hit seven billion people: over twice the number of people as when Boulding wrote his essay in 1966. Some believe it may reach ten billion by the end of this century.[10] There are few places on the Earth that a human has not set foot, and few places that with our technology and knowledge we could not feasibly live.

We're clearly not cowboys anymore. Humans have tamed the Wild West. Through our collective action we have learnt how to master and shape the Earth, and we can now see that it isn't as infinite or threatening as we first thought. This success, however, has come at a price. For our ancestors, the Earth was vast, but that vastness also signalled its abundance. Now we have grown in number and put our stamp in every corner, we can see that the Earth is actually startlingly limited. There are limits to the resources it can provide - whether water, food, land, oil, or anything else. Whereas the Earth was once too big to be safe, it is now too small compared to the burgeoning human population.

The limited resources available on the Earth have to be enough not just for the growing human race, but for all the other animals and plant life that share the planet as well. Our population growth might not be as significant an issue if we all consumed just what we needed to survive, but that has rarely been the human way. We cannot forget all that we have learnt and return to living like animals, or even like our ancestors in small, subsistence communities. The problem is that quite the opposite is occurring. As the overall human population grows, more and more people want to consume more and more resources, compounding the issue. People in places like China and India want to start to live and consume more, like we do here in Britain, and when we've enjoyed so much wealth for so long, it's hard to argue that they shouldn't.

So Boulding proposed that instead of seeing ourselves as cowboys, we are actually now more like astronauts, travelling through space on a spaceship Earth. Spaceships are isolated, delicately-balanced life-support machines, where all of the resources have to be carefully allocated to all of the crew. If they run out of food, astronauts can't just take a quick trip to the shops. They have to survive with whatever they have on board. Here on Earth, we now realise we live on a similarly isolated life-support machine. The Earth sustains us, but what is here is all that we have. There are not two Earths to make use of; just one. Whatever is here has to be used to sustain all of life, and has to be shared amongst all the astronauts. Much like on a spaceship, we have to get along with each other and learn to share our resources if we all want to survive. We also need to make sure we look after the spaceship Earth, and not damage its capacity to sustain life in the future.

Understanding the notion of 'spaceship Earth' has a huge consequence for how we operate almost every area of our society, our communities, and our economy. Humanity, in its masses, has become so populous and resource-hungry that we are damaging the capacity of the Earth to sustain life, including our own species. As we'll see in the next chapter, whilst there are some that still deny this is occurring, the overwhelming evidence supported by the vast majority of the scientists in this area points towards a sudden, unprecedented, human-caused change in the Earth's climatic conditions and life-supporting systems. It's clear that the issues of climate breakdown and resource use pose a huge threat to humanity, the scale and seriousness of which our politicians and governments show little sign of understanding or acting upon.

THE EARTH UNDER PRESSURE

POLITICAL POLICY-MAKING is, more often than not, short-term. Politicians and governments are more inclined to make decisions that ensure they stay in power and get elected next time around, rather than making long-term plans. However, environmental breakdown is a challenge that requires us to make plans for the *very* long term. Whilst we are experiencing, and will experience the consequences of climate change and resource scarcity in our lifetimes, the full impacts will not be felt by us, but by our children, grandchildren, and great grandchildren. Some might feel that this is all the more reason to act now; unfortunately this reasoning does not seem to be shared by our political leaders. The action required goes beyond recycling a bit, or using our cars less, or turning off lights when we leave the room. We need to make changes to our entire way of life. The way our societies and economies are constructed will need to be wholly and recognisably different.

It's quite possible that many people are put off of engaging with the issue by its scale; it's scary to acknowledge the size of our environmental impact and its consequences, and of the response required to resolve them. It's much easier to stick our heads in the sand and hope the science is wrong, or that some previously-unknown technology will suddenly turn up and save us just in time. We must also recognise that the huge changes needed might face self-interested opposition from those who have benefitted greatly from the way things are now – despite the many that have not thrived under the current system and may well prosper under a different one. It's also possible that there isn't action because not enough of us are fully aware of the extent of the problems.

Lots of people have learnt about 'global warming' at school, about CFCs (chlorofluorocarbons), the ozone layer and greenhouse gases, but those terms are rarely brought to life by translating them into 'what if?' scenarios. We've already mentioned that considering what we might want the future to look like is a good way of deciding on what policies to enact now; thinking through what the future *might* look like if we *don't* act can be equally useful. Asking 'what if?' is obviously a bit of a guessing game, but it is better to make an intelligent guess than to remain completely unprepared for the results of our actions. It's news to many people that climate breakdown and resource scarcity doesn't just mean things getting a bit warmer; our changing environment will have huge geopolitical and economic consequences.

This is because the distribution of people around the planet is related to the ability of that part of the planet to sustain human life. Most people in the world live in the Northern Hemisphere, where most of the land is, around a band of land north of the equator but south of the Arctic. It's not too hot in summer, and not too cold in winter. It rains enough to let crops grow, and with enough shrubbery for animals to graze. Within those regions, humanity groups into settlements around areas with a natural capacity to support them. There are few 'cities in the desert'. Instead humans form towns and villages along the coast, where there is ocean life to sustain them, or along rivers or in fertile valleys. The threat to humanity from the changing climate is thus not necessarily the temperature change itself – after all, we happily go on holiday somewhere warmer – but how the changing temperature and climate patterns affect the Earth's capacity to sustain humanity.

As the climate changes, land that once supported people may no longer do so, and the resulting hardship and displacement of people on our crowded planet will unavoidably lead to an increase in human conflict.[11] It's incredibly difficult to predict exactly when conflicts will occur and where, but it's not difficult to understand that they will. This impending reality appears to be largely ignored by those in power, although not in all cases: the US Military recently moved climate change towards the top of their list of national security threats.[12] As the journalist Gwynne Dyer, who has interviewed some of the world's leading climate scientists, economists, and military leaders for his book *Climate Wars*, concludes;

'...*for every degree that the average global temperature rises, so do the mass movements of population, the number of failed and failing states, and very probably the incidence of internal and international wars.*'[13]

So what exactly is happening to the climate that we need to be so wary of? Let's do a quick whistle-stop tour of the environmental issues to help put the extent of the challenges we face in context.

Global temperatures are increasing. They are increasing at an unprecedented rate. Data set after data set, compiled from measurements taken in all sorts of different ways show the same trend. This temperature increase strongly correlates with the rapidly increasing amount of greenhouse gases in the atmosphere, of which carbon dioxide (CO_2) is the most significant contributor. Greenhouse gases act as a layer in the atmosphere like glass does in a greenhouse, trapping the heat from the sun between itself and the Earth. CO_2 is increasing in the atmosphere because our industrialised (and industrialising) global economy is putting it there, mainly through burning fossil fuels for energy. We measure the amount of CO_2 in the atmosphere in parts-per-million (ppm), and the atmosphere, as of 2013, has just over 400ppm of CO_2 in it. It's a pretty meaningless figure on its own, but it's put in context a little bit when you consider that for the last million years or so the amount of CO_2 in the atmosphere never went outside of the 180ppm-280ppm range, and scientists believe the last time there was as much CO_2 in the atmosphere as there is now was over 4 million years ago, long before humans evolved.[14] The current amount of 400ppm is increasing by about 2ppm a year, and this rate of increase in carbon emissions is actually accelerating by about 3% each year (so this year we'll emit 3% more CO_2 than we did last year). This rapid increase in CO2 (and compared to anything pre-human it is very rapid indeed) is causing an increase in global temperature, which is measured against 1990 levels, the globally-agreed benchmark. While any increase in global temperature has negative impacts, scientists agree that the consequences of surpassing a 2^0C increase in temperature are particularly dire. The majority of climate scientists think that to avoid such an increase we need to limit carbon in the atmosphere to a maximum of 450ppm, which we're currently due to hit well before 2040, or in about 25 years[15] To consider the nature of that task, it means reducing global emissions by about 85% compared to 1990 levels, and unfortunately they are currently about 40% *above* levels in 1990.[16] Yet there are many who think that the 450ppm barrier is actually too optimistic, and that we shouldn't feel safe until we can bring CO_2 back down to below the 350ppm mark, where it last was in about 1990.[17] So we've not been making great progress. But why is this 2^0C figure so catastrophic? Well, it's the point at which climate scientists think there is a very good chance of consequences known as 'feedbacks' kicking in. Global temperature increases correspond closely to the amount of CO_2 and other greenhouse gases in the atmosphere, which means that as the CO_2 in the atmosphere increases, global temperature soon follows. Up to a certain point (the 2^0C figure mentioned earlier), should we stop emitting CO_2 in such vast quantities then the global temperature would, over a century or three, begin to decrease again.[18] The problem is that as CO_2 and the global temperature rises beyond that point, there's a high chance it will trigger a 'feedback' from other parts of the climate system that would keep the climate changing even if we subsequently reduce the amount of CO_2 we release into the atmosphere[19]. One example of a climate feedback is melting ice caps and snow cover.

Ice and snow is white and 'shiny' and the parts of the earth coated with it reflect large amounts of the Sun's heat back into the atmosphere. This helps keep the poles cool and the ice-sheets there stable. However, as the global temperature rises some ice melts, and melted ice-sheet turns into dark blue oceans which, instead of reflecting the Sun's heat, absorb it. The 'feedback' bit in this case occurs as the less ice and snow there is at the poles, the less chance the rest of it has of staying there. Melting ice leads to a darker sea surface that absorbs more of the Sun's heat, which leads to an increase in sea temperature and then to more ice melting. The speed at which the ice sheets are melting has led scientists to keep revising down the point in time when the Arctic will be completely free of sheet ice in the summer months. It's now thought that the Arctic is unlikely to have summer ice by 2020,[20] having reduced by an average of 18% in each of the last three decades.[21] In the Antarctic, summer ice is melting faster than at any point in the last 1,000 years[22].

Melting permafrost is a similar issue, but with a slightly different effect. Permafrost is completely frozen ground (below 0^0C, the freezing point of water) that occurs at high latitudes close to the poles. It is defined as ground where at least the top ten feet is frozen, but some can be frozen to a depth of over a kilometre. Permafrost currently covers about a quarter of the entire land surface of the Northern Hemisphere, but most of it is in areas so cold that we don't really go there or think about it. Permafrost isn't white and shiny and doesn't reflect the Sun's heat in the same way that arctic ice does, but it instead contains huge quantities of carbon and methane locked in amongst the frozen soil. As global temperatures increase, permafrost starts to thaw, releasing carbon dioxide and methane into the atmosphere.[23] CO_2 is bad enough, but methane, acting as a greenhouse gas, is between ten and twenty times as potent as CO_2 and so makes an even greater impact on increasing global temperatures.[24] The 'feedback' effect here happens where melting permafrost releases greenhouse gases, which in turn raise the global temperature, leading to more melting permafrost.

Another feedback results from ocean acidification. The oceans store huge amounts of carbon, and as part of the carbon-cycle they naturally 'soak up' the excess carbon in the atmosphere. The problem is not only that the more CO_2 the oceans hold, the less they are able to soak up in future, but much like the 'fizz' in a soft drink or a glass of lager, the warmer the oceans the less CO_2 (or fizz) they can hold. The oceans have already absorbed half of all human-produced carbon dioxide,[25] but there are concerns that as the oceans warm, they would become less of a CO_2 sink and more of a CO_2 source, relinquishing some of their long-held carbon and becoming a net emitter of carbon dioxide. The seabed also contains methane, which, in a similar way to permafrost, is released as the oceans warm. These released greenhouse gases would continue increasing the planet's temperature irrespective of continuing human emissions, whilst the increasing acidity of the ocean waters (fizzy drinks are acidic) causes significant damage to marine ecosystems, with knock-on effects for what is an essential element of the global food supply.[26]

If the global temperature continues to rise past 2°C then regardless of how much of our CO_2 emissions we manage to cut – or even if we stop emitting CO_2 altogether – the feedback processes we have set in motion by this time will keep changing the climate in ways we have no control over. We're realising that the Earth's systems are actually quite delicately balanced, and we're in real danger of tipping them over the edge. The triggering of climate feedbacks is sometimes called 'runaway' climate change; pushing a cart to the top of a hill requires effort, but once it's there, it will run down the other side again all on its own. The UN's Fourth Report of the Intergovernmental Panel on Climate Change (IPCC) puts it clearly. According to the report, should feedbacks be triggered then man-made 'warming and sea level rise would continue for centuries due to the time scales associated with climate processes and feedbacks, even if GHG (Greenhouse Gases) concentrations were to be stabilised'.[27]

Yet the question remains: why should we care if the global temperature increases? It's a legitimate question to ask for anyone shivering away in the snow waiting for a bus on a workday morning, in the middle of a drearily grey, Northern Hemisphere winter. For them, the notion of 'global warming' sounds inviting rather than alarming. For the majority of the world however, the effects of climate change will be anything other than pleasant.

One consequence is that, as the First Law of Thermodynamics suggests, a warmer climate equates to more energy in the Earth's weather systems, and we can thus expect more extreme and violent weather and higher-energy storms.[28] This is bad news for everyone, but especially for those people living closer to the tropics (where temperatures are higher and storms generally more violent anyway), those living in river valleys and flood plains, and those in low-lying coastal areas. The latter point is particularly pertinent when combined with rising sea levels; if you happen to live in a low-lying coastal area on a flood plain near the tropics (New Orleans, Bangladesh) then now would be a good time to sell-up. Those of us living in more temperate latitudes can still expect more extreme fluctuations in weather. As the UK government's chief scientist Professor Sir John Beddington warned:

'The [current] variation we are seeing in temperature or rainfall is double the rate of the average. That suggests that we are going

to have more droughts, we are going to have more floods, we are going to have more sea surges and we are going to have more storms'.[29]

Closely related to this is the way in which rising temperatures are affecting seasonal weather patterns. We're learning more about this as it happens, and we now know that changes to ocean temperature and the melting of the polar ice caps are changing the historical position of the jet stream: a current of air in the atmosphere that meanders between hot and cold air-masses, and determines what weather is experienced in Western Europe and North America. The change in climatic conditions is causing the jet stream to move around less, depositing consistent weather over a large area for longer periods of time. Where previously much of Western Europe, including Britain, has experienced calm, changeable weather, with doses of mild and bearable sunshine regularly interspersed with rain, we can now expect an increase in extreme, extended weather patterns. These new patterns will lead to much more regular instances of flooding in some areas, and droughts in others.[30]

Another consequence is that the hotter, more arid climate and unpredictable weather will reduce the overall land available for agriculture. If the global temperature were to increase by 2^0C, this would actually mean a smaller increase over the oceans and coastal areas, but a much greater increase of perhaps as much as 4^0C or 5^0C in the middle of the large landmasses. Unfortunately the middle of the continents, especially the huge grain-producing regions of the central USA, Canada, and China, are where a substantial proportion of the world's food and cereal crop is grown. Similarly, many major food-producing regions such as the Nile valley in Africa and the Indus basin in Pakistan, (the largest single area of irrigated farmland in the world), are likely to suffer from a decrease in their water supply. The Indus valley system relies on three rivers that are supplied by melt-water from glaciers high up in the Himalayan mountain range. Increasing temperatures are causing these glaciers to recede. As this happens, these vast tracts of irrigated farmland, producing food for hundreds of millions of people, could run short of water. As well as this, other countries that are already 'hot', e.g. those in North Africa (Morocco, Egypt), Southern Europe (Spain, Portugal), and Central America (Mexico), will become more arid as temperatures rise, increasing desertification and reducing crop yields.[31] Crop yields are just as heavily affected, if not more so, by extreme weather events than average increases in temperature. Farmers are already fighting against more frequent and severe droughts and are unable to prepare for all the unusual types and variations of weather that now occur, and that will occur in future.[32, 33] As a result, crops are damaged or lost and harvests are ruined.[34, 35] A recent report by the World Bank into the effects of climate change on the world's poorest regions highlighted how a two-degree increase in global temperatures could lead to a 20% reduction in the availability of fresh water, with devastating consequences for food production.[36] Similarly, a groundbreaking report by the Centre for Low Carbon Futures finds that the impacts of climate change on food production will be keenly felt within just ten years, and that 'the increased drought risk is an imminent threat to food security on a global scale.'[37]

Throw an increasing (and increasingly demanding) global population into the mix alongside warmer and ever more volatile weather, and it's easy to see why the already strained global food supply is likely to come under increasing pressure, reflected in rapidly increasing food prices. Considering the diversion of more and more grain crops from food use to biofuel production,[38] as well as the inflationary effects of food-price speculation from a rampant financial sector (we'll examine this in more detail later), it quickly becomes apparent that we are facing not an inconvenience, but a crisis.[39] It might initially be bearable for us in the richer parts of the world, but for the roughly three billion people on the planet living on less than three dollars a day, just the food-price increases alone are, and will be, devastating. This is without considering the other climate-related effects on their lives and livelihoods, which they are ill-equipped to adjust to.[40] Fully understanding the extent and severity of the consequences of climate change is critical, not just for strengthening public and political will for preventative action, but for contingency planning for those consequences that now seem unavoidable. To predict the direct physical consequences of climate change is challenging, and includes a significant margin of uncertainty. The secondary consequences of how communities and nations will be affected by climate change, and how they might respond to the crises it generates, are even harder to determine. A number of commentators have made educated guesses at what some of these consequences might be, with the acknowledgement that much of the relative peace and cooperation between nations in the past fifty years has been the result of wealth and plentiful resources.[41] Climate change and continuing population growth is now ending this. We can expect a reduction in the global trade in food and fuel as more nations seek to hold on to the resources they do have. India, for example, has already implemented bans on exporting its key staple rice, in an attempt to keep prices down so that its own citizens can afford to eat. Following a heat wave and poor harvest in 2010, the Russian government banned the exporting of grain, leading to a food price spike on international markets, and ultimately food riots across Africa and Asia.[42] Nations will have to become more self-sufficient, yet this will be a difficult task where populations are growing, security is disturbed, and climate change is damaging food production capacity. We should expect more famines, greater human migrations, the closing of previously-open borders, an increase in conflicts, and increased stresses placed on governments and societies. The eroding of national governance is likely to undermine global cooperation on climate change, adding what could be considered to be 'geopolitical feedbacks' to the climatic ones, and exacerbating the problems countries will face. The breakdown of law and order is not conducive to considered, long-term policy planning.

If, as now seems likely, we do trigger climate feedbacks, then the levels of anthropogenic warming we could expect over subsequent centuries as predicted by the UN's IPCC would make a 2^{0}C increase seem tame by comparison. A 3^{0}C to 5^{0}C global increase, which would mean much higher increases in the middle of continents, could completely re-shape the productive profile of the Earth's land and, as a result, could be reasonably expected to transform the distribution of humanity across the entire planet. How and in what shape human civilisation will survive this kind of upheaval is anyone's guess; so is the continuing habitability of a planet whose life-support systems will have been so comprehensively overwhelmed. There is also a chance that even the best guesses of these impacts could be underestimates. Recent analysis of undisturbed lake sediments laid down when the Earth's atmosphere last contained the levels of greenhouse gases we have today show that the global temperature was eight degrees warmer than it is today, and the sea level was *forty* metres higher.[43] James Lovelock, the grandfather of modern climate science, wrote in the *Independent* newspaper in 2007 that he believed that by the end of the century the temperature will be five degrees hotter in the tropics, eight degrees hotter in temperate regions, much of the land in tropical areas will become scrub and desert, and billions of humans will perish.[44] These views might be towards the extreme end of the scientific spectrum, but when such an eminent scientist starts talking about the survival of humanity in terms of 'breeding pairs' then it should, at the very least, start alarm bells ringing.

It's fair to ask how our politicians and governments are confronting these unique and critical issues. After all, we're not talking about a mere inconvenience, but the biggest challenge to ever face organised humanity. We are changing our planet to the point where a global human civilisation as we know it may struggle to survive. We cannot be 100% sure of this doomsday scenario at this stage; what we do know is that our best estimates predict that we will make our Earth an incredibly dangerous place for humanity. When the stakes are that high is it really worth the risk of continuing without making significant changes to how we live?

In a BBC television programme broadcast in 2008,[45] an employee at an observatory in Hawaii posed an interesting thought experiment. After many years of looking at the stars and searching for signals of alien life with no success, he outlined a startling view. With the incomprehensible size and age of the universe, and the trillions and trillions of planets that could harbour life, and by extrapolating the known statistics, the universe should be literally teeming with proof of artificial intelligence. He suggested that the reason for this absence of life was that the development of intelligent life to the stage where humans are now was so rapid (in evolutionary timescales), that in every instance they were able to completely destroy themselves and their planet before they developed the collective capability to live within the limits of their immediate environment. This would make incidences of intelligent life, rather than a statistical certainty throughout the universe, simply the tiniest of momentary blips in the grand arc of evolution. It might sound far-fetched but, of the billions of years of life on this planet, humanity has only had the power to significantly alter the natural systems of the planet on which it relies for a few hundred of them. That it might take us little longer to render the planet almost uninhabitable for ourselves is a fascinating and sobering thought.

A LACK OF PROGRESS

FACED WITH THE NATURE and size of this global challenge, the human response so far has been completely inadequate. Despite the 1997 Kyoto agreement (ratified by almost all countries, with the USA and Canada the significant exceptions), which put targets on reducing global greenhouse gas emissions, we still live in a world that emits increasing levels of greenhouse gas almost every year. Carbon emissions are now rising faster than they were in 1990, with no sign of change. Despite advances in renewable technology, rising global demand for energy means that we are still finding new ways to damage the environment in the pursuit of more fossil fuels through technologies such as hydraulic fracturing, or 'fracking', and the extraction of unconventional oil from tar sands.[46]

Governments in the world's major economies have identified but then consistently failed to tackle the issues, often talking up their green credentials but then neglecting to act on the scientific evidence.[47] Our current coalition government in Britain, despite starting off by declaring itself the 'greenest government ever' has gone backwards on green policies since 2010.[48, 49, 50] It has actively encouraged more fossil fuel extraction through beneficial tax policies,[51] and in 2011 closed the Sustainable Development Commission whose purpose was to 'hold government to account to ensure the needs of society, the economy, and the environment were properly balanced in the decisions it made and the way it ran itself'.[52] In 2012 the world's largest economy, the USA, went through its biggest presidential election ever without either candidate once mentioning climate change or other environmental issues in significant debate during the months of campaigning.[53] It is perhaps no surprise then that international cooperation has fared little better. Successive UN climate change conferences have failed to yield any meaningful agreement on how to tackle the issue, with developed countries often facing off against developing ones, and entrenched, self-serving positions yielding little during what can be days of negotiations.[54]So why can't we bring about the changes that we need to? This challenge is uniquely ours. Previous generations didn't know about this crisis, and future generations will arrive too late to act. The implication is that we are the only generation that have both the knowledge and the time to respond; that's some responsibility. Yet the population of the Earth is still growing at a rapid rate, and we are consuming ever more resources than before, releasing ever more carbon into the atmosphere, and moving dangerously close to triggering runaway changes to our environmental systems that we will then have little chance of halting or reversing.

One of the reasons for the lack of progress made might be that politicians and governments think they wouldn't get elected again if they tried to implement the difficult policies necessary to stop climate change. There is no doubt an element of truth to this. Policies that affect our perceived short-term prosperity or make such significant changes to the way people live are likely to cause some consternation amongst at least some of the population. The problem with this view though is that it assumes that politicians aren't willing at all to make decisions that might make them unpopular. A quick look at some recent policies shows this to be untrue. The current British government for example has made unpopular decisions about economic austerity including cuts to public services and changes to pensions, despite the fact that these decisions have led to marches on the streets and a rapid decline in the government's potential voting share. It has done this because, for whatever reason, it believes this to be the 'correct' thing to do. If unpopular decisions can be made on issues like public spending, then there's no reason why they can't be made regarding the environment.

Another reason why progress isn't made in tackling climate change is that it doesn't make very good TV. When we live in a world of instant information, breaking news, and the easily digested sound-bite, an issue which arises almost imperceptibly slowly and whose greatest effects might only be felt decades from now will find it hard to compete with more immediate challenges. As wonderfully outlined in the seminal book *Futureshock* by Alvin Toffler,[55] our culture and society operate on increasingly short timescales. Making long-term decisions based on long-term projections for the benefit of people who might not even be alive yet is a difficult sell. Again though, this argument isn't completely watertight. Not only is it the job of politicians to lead from the front in identifying what issues are of national importance, and then put them on the national radar as appropriate, but they are also very capable of taking long-term decisions. The discussions and planning for the replacement of the British nuclear weapon system, Trident, started years ago, yet it will cost tens of *billions* of pounds and isn't due to be delivered until 2028. Likewise, the new HS2 high-speed rail line will cost £35bn, and will not be fully finished until 2032. In addition, governments make decisions about energy policy that look to accurately meet energy needs decades into the future. Nuclear power stations, which require long-term government spending commitments, have a lifespan of thirty or forty years,[56] and create as a by-product highly radioactive material that has to be buried for a period of time somewhere between a century and a millennium. Governments are clearly capable of making, and making the case for, long-term decisions.

It might also be that more hasn't been done because there is a belief that the science is still uncertain, and that this uncertainty weakens the resolve to make changes. Unfortunately there are powerful people and groups with a vested interest in sowing seeds of doubt about climate change, probably because they stand to lose out financially if governments take difficult policy decisions to combat it.[57] For example, recent studies have shown that if we were to stick to carbon reduction targets then up to 80% of fossil fuel reserves we know about would have to be left in the ground, potentially costing energy companies £4 *trillion*.[58] Yet it would be bizarre to prioritise the short-term future of energy companies over the long-term future of the entire human race, and it doesn't change the facts about the situation we face: a situation which is plain to see for anyone who wishes to take the time to learn more about it.[59]

There is also a policy of 'balance' in some news organisations, which feel they have to represent both sides of an argument fairly, even if one side is an overwhelming minority, as is the case of those who refute the existence of climate change. This kind of balance might make sense in some areas, where there are significant schools of thought that still hold opposing views, but it makes little sense for climate change, where a recent study showed that 99.5% of peer-reviewed environmental scientists think that climate change is real and that humans are causing it.[60]

31

For those who are still in some way unconvinced by the vast majority of scientific opinion, the climate journalist Gwynne Dyer makes an important point;

'There must remain some infinitesimal possibility that the sceptics are right and everybody else is wrong, but the evidence for global warming caused by human activities is so strong that urgent action is required. The potential cost of doing too little, too late is vastly greater than the cost that might be incurred by doing more to fight global warming than turns out, at some later date, to have been strictly necessary'.[61]

This is not to say that there is no uncertainty around the climate issue. Whilst science is agreed on the existence of the problem and its source, and how dangerous it is, there are also aspects that are less clear. Attempts to make projections based on such a massive and complex system are unavoidably susceptible to some degree of uncertainty or margin for error, especially when we have no historical precedent for the kind of impact we are currently making on our planet. Yet research has shown that the models used for climate science and the predictions they have made have proved remarkably accurate, and the majority of newly emerging evidence points towards the worst-case scenarios of prior predictions, rather than minimising them.[62, 63, 64] That we have to act soon is therefore not in question. To paraphrase a common quote, it's better to be roughly right than precisely wrong.

The obstacle of economic growth

Perhaps the main reason for lack of progress is economics: the idea that taking the steps necessary to respond to climate changes will create economic hardship, or won't be economically feasible. One of the main complications is that of economic growth. In our current economic models, it's believed that there is a bleak future for society unless there is an increase in the goods and services produced each year, from one year to the next. The amount of goods and services produced in a given year is measured in Gross Domestic Product, or GDP.

Explaining why it is perceived that we always have to pursue economic growth is a little complicated, but we'll go through it step by step, using companies that produce metal components as an example. In our current economic model we invest in machines and better technology in order to produce things more efficiently, so we can 'outperform' our competitors. If Company A produces components more efficiently than Company B, for example, it means that Company A can make components at a lower cost than Company B, either by making them quicker and so using less labour (fewer 'man-hours' in total), or by using cheaper or fewer materials during the production process. Because they cost less to make, Company A can therefore sell its components at a lower price than Company B and still make the same amount of profit. As a result it will likely sell more components than Company B. Alternatively, it can sell components at the same price as Company B and make more profit, and so have more money to reinvest in becoming even more efficient. Either way, over a period of time, and in a 'competitive' market place, (and ignoring complicating factors like how good each company is at advertising), Company A is going to end up richer and more successful because of its higher efficiency. It's possible that Company B could even be driven out of business.

So far, so good; after all, there's nothing wrong with increasing efficiency is there? Well, there's nothing *wrong* as such, but to increase efficiency (making something for a lower cost) you have to spend less to make it. One of the biggest costs of making things is the cost of employing people: what economists call 'labour'. People cost money to employ, so if you can replace them with machines, or otherwise make processes more efficient so you don't have to employ as many people, then you'll make more profit. The problem with this is that unemployment is debilitating and people need jobs, so if you want to increase efficiency and still keep the same number of jobs, you have no choice but to make more stuff.[65] However, there's no point making more stuff if you can't sell it, so there have to be people with enough money to spend to be able to buy it. The only way that's going to happen is if people have jobs and good wages. You can hopefully see where this is going. The realisation dawns that our entire capitalist economy is built on a rather delicately-balanced cycle, entirely reliant on the global community making and consuming more and more stuff.

We've established throughout this chapter that making and consuming increasingly more stuff is destroying the capacity of our planet to sustain life, and at an increasing rate. We appear to have hit an impasse. On one hand our economic system requires constant 'growth' to provide livelihoods, yet on the other this growth will eventually lead to a desperate human existence on a decaying, depleted Earth; points we will revisit later in this book. When politicians are faced with this challenge, it's no wonder they are far happier to pay it lip-service and just pretend to engage, rather than articulating and wrestling with the severity of the problem. In the end they resort to what they know: pursuing the growth mantra that seems to have worked well for the last few decades, and trying to ignore the other side of the equation.

Politicians also convince themselves that growth is the most important thing because of the neoliberal view of global 'competition' between countries. Much like Company A and Company B, they believe Britain is in competition with other countries, and if we don't become more efficient we might 'go bust', or become weak, poor, and vulnerable. This whole competition is frequently described as a global 'race',[66] or even an 'economic war'.[67] Quite where we're racing to, or whether anybody can ever 'win' is never really analysed; nor is the question of whether the world we create in the process of trying to win is somewhere we'd actually like to live. We certainly don't talk about what life is like, or has been like, for the 'losers', or whether they deserve it. The point of the competition narrative is that we all just need to get our heads down and work as hard as we can. Only then may we stand a chance of maintaining or improving our place in the world, and damn the consequences.

From within the neoliberal competition narrative the future looks grim, especially as successive economic forecasts have consistently overstated the likely success of our economy, and government policies still perceive a decade of 'austerity'.[68] [69] [70] So what hope is there? In the middle of this mess it seems that we are a long way from becoming the Astronauts that we need to be.

It appears that we have become completely dependent on a system that is taking us to ruin. It's reasonable to ask why more hasn't been done to change this. I don't think there is any one answer, but it's likely to be a combination of the answers listed above, as well as the fact that few people really have any idea what can be done about it. Where there have been some answers, they are often seen as too politically improbable to even get started on, or they appear to create more problems than they solve. We're in an incredibly dangerous position, and we seem incapable of getting ourselves out of it. That's the bleak bit, but over the course of the rest of this book we'll find that there are genuine, practical choices that we can make to reform our economy and society, and that can help us prevent the destruction of the capacity of our planet to sustain human civilisation.

Maybe one of the reasons why there is no apparent way forward is that we haven't been willing to examine the issues from a wide enough angle. We live in a country that, like most of the countries in the world, has a 'capitalist' economic system. That means that there is private ownership of land and of the means to produce goods and services, and that these private enterprises are managed in such a way as to be able to engage with other enterprises in a market in the pursuit of profit. It is an economic system which accommodates individual property and economic decision-making in order for those individuals to be able to get richer. An economic system is not the same as a political system, and capitalist economies have successfully existed in all sorts of different political systems, from Fascist (inter-war Italy), Communist (current-day China), Autocratic (many South America countries in the 1970s and 80s) to Social Democracies (in current-day Western Europe).

If the world is viewed from within the capitalist cycle of ever increasing consumption, with the rules and tools that it provides, then unless the solution can be found from within that system there can be no way forward. What if in order to find a way forward we need to look outside that system, away from what is familiar? What if we need to move away from the kinds of stories and language that fill today's newspapers and economic and social commentary, and re-examine the core values and beliefs that our economic system is built upon? The aim is not revolution. It is instead a wider acknowledgment that our capitalist system itself does not have a solution to the damaging impact that it has had, in its current form, on the Earth. A system that, when faced with a disease of growth and overconsumption in a world of limited resources, can prescribe only more growth is a system that has clearly run out of ideas.[71]Capitalism in our current age means more than just how we order our economies. It hints at how money has become a totem of sorts in our society. We measure the success of our country almost exclusively in terms of economic indicators like GDP, and struggle to agree on the value of anything unless we can put a price tag on it.[72] The logic behind this is simple: the more things that have a price tag, the more that can be bought and sold, and therefore become privately owned. We understand this almost inherently, and although we may sense that this shouldn't have to be the case, it is so embedded in society that it is hard to imagine that it could have ever been different. Yet different it was. In *Ill fares the land*, political historian Tony Judt highlighted just how recently this kind of thinking had become commonplace, and attributed it to political decisions taken in just the last fifty years, such as mass privatisations and policies that placed the political emphasis on the individual at the expense of wider society.

'As recently as the 1970s, the idea that the point of life was to get rich and that governments existed to facilitate this would have been ridiculed: not only by capitalism's traditional critics but also by many of its staunchest defenders. Relative indifference to wealth for its own sake was widespread in the post-war decades. In a survey of English schoolboys taken in 1949, it was discovered that the more intelligent the boy the more likely he was to choose an interesting career at a reasonable wage over a job that would merely pay well. Today's schoolchildren and college students can imagine little else but the search for a lucrative job'.[73]

Political commentary at every level is now almost always framed by two things: the desire for greater economic 'efficiency', meaning spending less money and making more, and the continual need for economic growth. The pursuit of these aims continues to the extent that almost every other goal or objective, however beneficial, is checked against, and made subservient to, its effect on GDP. Faced with governing and social systems that place economic concerns above all others, the first step to understanding the choices we have is to understand more about what money is, how economies work, and the role wealth plays in our lives.[74] Only then will we be able to realise what we can change and how, and be free to be able to think about all the other things that shape the world that we want ourselves and our children to be able to inhabit.

THE CAKE

EVERYONE WANTS TO BE RICH, including me. I'm fortunate (at the time of writing at least) to have a good job and get paid every month, which covers my bills and allows me to have a bit more left over to spend on 'fun' things, like clothes and music and a few meals out. Yet I'd still like a bit more money, so I could go on more expensive holidays, or have a nicer car. 'Just a little bit more money and I'll be happy', I tell myself. Yet is it money that I really want? Or the things that money can buy? Or is it something else entirely?

Imagine I had a million pounds sitting on the floor in a box. I might think that I'm rich. But what if it was in an impenetrable, locked box that self-destructed if I attempted to open it? I might have a million pounds, but if I could never spend it, I wouldn't be rich any more. So money in itself doesn't make us rich. It's spending it that does; it's having the things that money can buy us, whether that's new clothes, or nice food, a big house or two, or a luxurious holiday.

Now let's think through another idea. Imagine that at a given moment the money that everyone in the world had suddenly doubled. Would we all be twice as rich? The answer, I'm afraid, is 'No'. Even though we now had double the amount of money as before, there wouldn't suddenly be double the amount of stuff for us to buy with it. Money is only worth as much as the real stuff we can exchange it for. In this theoretical example, if the amount of stuff available to buy had stayed the same whilst our money doubled, then our money would only be worth half as much as it was before.[75] Money is subject to exactly the same rule of scarcity as any other object: the rule that explains why grains of sand are less valuable than diamonds. Diamonds are undoubtedly prettier, but they wouldn't be worth very much if there were trillions of them on every beach.

The amount of real stuff we can buy is constrained by how much we can produce. What, and how much, we can produce (and consume, and therefore how wealthy we are) is actually determined by just three things: the materials and resources we have, the number and skills of the people we can put to work, and the amount of technology we have and how we use it. Each of these things is startlingly limited, although the first two to a greater degree than the last. This point is either ignored or unrepresented in public discussions about our current economic and environmental situation. We rarely talk about the natural limits that our economies must operate within.

Over the last fifty years in developed countries we've become wealthier because we've built mines, oilrigs and factories, dug up more stuff, and turned it into things we didn't have before. As a result we now have washing machines and refrigerators and cars and lots of shiny digital bits. Another reason why we've become so much richer during this period, however, is that lots and lots of other people on the planet haven't. We've had the lion's share of the planet's resources to ourselves. The entire population of sub-Saharan Africa, over five-hundred million people living on a land area twice the size of Europe, has seen barely any increase in individual wealth in the last fifty years, despite their lands contributing many of the resources that have driven our own wealth in the UK.[76] Even just twenty years ago the people of China, (a country of a billion people), were only half as wealthy as Britain, (a country of just sixty million). By 2012 however, whilst the average Briton still consumed more than the average Chinese, China as a country had sped past

Britain in terms of total consumption.[77] With more and more of the world's previously under-developed populations in places like China and India laying claim to the Earth's resources, it is hardly surprising that the large expansion in wealth witnessed in the West during the second half of the last century appears to have ground to a halt.

There is another reason that our wealth cannot keep increasing. As we explored briefly in the first few chapters, we are not just reaching the limit of the Earth's capacity to sustain our current way of life, but we have completely surpassed it. Scientists have determined a measure for how much food, water, and other resources the Earth's land can produce, as well as its ability to re-process our wastes, and have called these 'global hectares'. If we were to share our resources evenly, then there are a little less than two global hectares available for each person living on the Earth. However, in the UK and the rest of Western Europe, we use about five global hectares per person, and in other places in the world the figure is even higher: people in the USA and Australia use, on average, about ten each.[78] At our current level of consumption we would therefore need almost two Earth's worth of productive land to sustain us indefinitely into the future. Scientists estimate that the point that we passed the 'one Earth' mark of consumption was about 1970. We're living on borrowed time; a single space-ship Earth cannot keep everyone on it at the same high level of wealth to which a relatively small number of us have become accustomed.

Most of the time, when our politicians and the media discuss wealth and economics they either don't acknowledge, or don't understand, that these limits exist. They think that we're cowboys when actually we're all astronauts. A world without limits means we can all get richer and richer forever, and we can all own our own yachts or football clubs, live the Hollywood lifestyle and drink expensive champagne. A limited world, however, like the real one we actually live in, is a very different prospect. It's a lot like a cake, and everyone in the world wants a slice. We can slice it up in lots of different ways, we can take pieces and swap them around, but we're not going to suddenly end up with two cakes. Not all seven billion people on the planet can own a hundred-acre estate, an energy company, or a football club.

Over time someone will find another oil field, or develop a new technology, and the size of the cake may grow a small amount, yet planetary limits are making any expansion harder and harder. As discussed before, over time there are more people on the planet and also more of them who, driven either by advertising, a misplaced sense of entitlement, or the desire to meet their basic needs and escape crushing poverty, want to acquire larger slices of the cake. We could double the amount of money in everyone's bank account, but it would make no difference to everyone's wealth. The cake is, more or less, the cake, and it's simply not big enough to satisfy the demands of everyone based on current levels of consumption. Because of this, it is the amount of money a person has in relation to others, rather than their absolute amount, that determines whether they can access the resources required for survival.[79] To use an example, someone who earned $5 in a world where everyone else only earned $2 would be able to secure a larger proportion of the cake than someone who earned $10 in a world where everyone else earned the same.

The dominance of humanity on a limited Earth is the global and environmental backdrop to the economic challenges that we currently face in the UK. We live in a world of finite resources, divided between increasing amounts of people. We have been living well beyond the capacity of the Earth to continually sustain us, and we are now beginning to experience the pressures that result. GDP might edge up a bit over the coming years, but we're unlikely to be able to consume much more than we have done in the recent past. By the current definition of what it means to be wealthy, in twenty or thirty years' time we won't be much richer, and we may even be poorer, than we are today. [80]

Unfortunately, as we have discussed, the political response to these challenges demonstrates little, if any, recognition of their imminence and severity. Our political leaders instead appear to be carrying on as normal, by implementing the same neoliberal policies that have dominated for the last thirty years: privatisation, lower taxes for big corporations, and the removal of regulation. In fact, looking at government policy, you'd be forgiven for failing to notice that the environmental crisis even exists. Policy seems to be formed under the shadow of the 'financial crisis': the 2007/08 banking shock and subsequent global recession that much of the UK population is still suffering from over half a decade later, despite a recent return to overall GDP growth. [81] As a result of the financial crisis, the government is enacting huge cuts to spending known as 'austerity', with the stated intention of trying to boost the economy. [82] Few sessions of Prime Ministers Questions at the House of Commons go by without the spectre of the crisis being raised as an excuse for either government action or inaction on at least one point of debate. The political emphasis on economic growth drowns out any consideration of the Earth's natural limits, or of the policies we would need to live within them.

Because of the impact the financial crisis has on government policy, we need to gain a better understanding of it if we are to be able to offer an alternative economic response. We will need to understand how our financial system works, and how we've ended up with the austerity policies that we are attempting to endure. By looking in more detail at our economy, and the role that money plays within it, we can establish that it is possible for our economic and financial systems to be ordered in a way that enables us to live sustainably. We will see that we have the economic tools we need to provide a safe, stable, and prosperous future, should we find the political will to use them.

THE FINANCIAL CRISIS

THE COLLAPSE in 2008 of the US Investment Bank Lehmann Brothers, following a run on the Northern Rock building society in the UK a year earlier, marked the beginning of what we now call the 'financial crisis'. This is the term used to describe the economic problems that unfolded in most Western economies from 2007-08, aspects of which still carry on in various forms today. Other terms sometimes used are the 'financial crash' or the 'credit crunch'.

There were lots of different, yet connected causes for the crisis, but the collapse of such a huge global bank as Lehmann Brothers drew the world's attention to a trend in financial services (the collective term for banks, loan companies, mortgage companies, insurers, and financial investment companies) for ever greater risk-taking.[83] This risk-taking, driven by a culture of huge bonuses and individual financial rewards, involved selling and trading financial products such as mortgages and loans, with little concern for how these would be repaid or whether they were financially sustainable. There was a collective blind-spot across the industry, where everyone seemed to believe that the good times would go on forever and that the financial markets would sort out any potential danger by 'spreading the risk around'.[84] It turned out that the markets were doing no such thing, and the increasingly risky trading, combined with a lack of effective government oversight and regulation of the sector put many financial companies in a precarious position.[85, 86] The culture of excessive risk-taking in banking was led by an increase in 'speculation'. Speculation is gambling on the price of products changing over time, so that by buying now and selling later (or the other way around) traders can make lots of money in a short period of time. It's a more risky activity for a bank than traditional banking activities such as taking deposits and issuing personal loans, but the potential profits are much higher. For much of the last century, there were regulations that placed restrictions on what certain financial institutions could and couldn't do. Traditional savings banks were allowed to take deposits and issue loans, but not to speculate. Speculation was reserved for investment banks and other kinds of financial institutions. However, towards the end of the last century there was a trend towards the deregulation of finance, with the 'Big-Bang' deregulation in Britain in 1986, the de-mutualisation of building societies in the 1990's and, in the USA, the 1999 rescinding of the Glass-Steagall Act,[87] among others. These changes removed the barriers between different kinds of financial institutions, allowing building societies to become banks, savings banks to start speculating, and other financial institutions to provide traditional banking services.

This had two impacts. Firstly, it meant that people's savings and deposits, and the banking services needed to run the day-to-day economy, became mixed up with the gambles that the speculative side of the banks were making in the search for bigger and quicker profits. Secondly, it meant that money that would previously have been used to invest in the real economy by being lent to businesses to develop their products and processes was instead being diverted to the riskier but more profitable cause of speculation. Much of this diverted money was used for trading in strange financial products known as derivatives. Derivatives are financial products that are 'derived' from existing products, such as a mortgage. They can be made up of debt, or insurance policies taken against that debt, or contracts on future prices or exchange rates, or a combination of these that are bought and sold on a market. Many of them are very complex, and this means it's difficult to tell what they are really worth, or whether allowing them to be traded is good or bad for the wider economy.

If you're unsure as to how debt can be traded, then it's best to imagine debt as a little factory, or as a shop or other business, that produces regular amounts of money for whoever owns it. If Person A takes out a £100,000 mortgage then the mortgage company or bank that gave it to Person A owns that debt, and in return they receive Person A's monthly mortgage payments. For the bank or mortgage company, Person A's regular payment is in effect an income for them owning that debt. They see buying this debt as an investment much like any other. They could have bought a factory or shop but instead they bought some debt, and in the same way they expect a regular income in return. When the debt is traded and another company buys it, the ownership changes hands, and that company will receive Person A's monthly mortgage payment instead.

One of the factors that gave the financial crisis its truly global reach was the uncertainty around some of the fancy new derivatives known as asset-backed securities, or 'securities' for short. These are big lumps of debt, made up of lots of different types of debt such as mortgages or car loans that individually might be too small to trade on the international market. In order to make them tradable they are bundled together, or 'securitised', into bigger packages and then sold on in bulk. Unfortunately, when securities were packaged and sold on, they often contained both high-quality debt (if Richard Branson was to borrow £100 from me for a week, I'm fairly sure he'd be able to repay it) and debt that was low quality. Low-quality debt is riskier and might have a higher chance of default, which means the borrower would not be able to repay. How likely debt is to be repaid is reflected in its interest rate: how much it costs to pay it back. Some traders took good quality and bad quality debt, and mixed them together before selling them on. These securities were then mixed again with others and resold, and on and on, until no-one really knew the quality of debt these packages contained.

The trigger for the crisis was a large and fairly sudden fall in house prices in the US housing market in 2008. This sudden fall was the bursting of a bubble of unrealistically high prices that had built up based upon the easy supply of money for mortgages, caused by the excessive risk-taking and lending from banks, as well as the over-confidence from many people about the strength of the economy. Borrowers believed that the economy would keep on growing, that house prices would continue to rise and that their jobs would be secure, and so they took mortgages out on houses that they really couldn't afford to buy. This was called the 'sub-prime' housing market. When changes in borrowers' financial circumstances meant they couldn't keep paying back their mortgages, they were evicted from their homes, which were repossessed by the mortgage lender. When the 'bubble burst', the increase in the number of available houses (an increase in supply) combined with a decrease in the number of people who could afford houses (a decrease in demand), causing house prices to plummet.

As a result of this housing market bubble bursting, a number of things happened that put the financial system at risk. Firstly, when people stopped paying their mortgages, banks lost the certainty of that future income. Secondly, because of the drop in house prices, the banks found that the houses that they now owned through repossession weren't worth as much as they were when they were purchased, and so the banks lost some of the value of their initial loan. Thirdly, financial institutions all over the world that held securities containing US mortgage debt suddenly realised that these products weren't worth as much as they thought they were. It turned out that a lot of these securities had been over-priced, and that they were rated as high-quality debt when in fact they were made up of some high-quality debt, but combined with a lot of risky, low-quality, sub-prime debt as well.

Unfortunately once the financial crisis began to bite, the banks - who borrow from each other on a daily basis as part of the banking system - started to lose confidence in the ability of each other to pay back any loans. This was compounded by the uncertainty over how much banks had actually lost through speculating on financial products, because no one really knew what the products were actually worth. As this confidence seeped away, the banks simply stopped lending to one another, (as well as other businesses that needed overdrafts or short-term loans), and the whole system ground to a halt. The banks that before the crisis could have borrowed themselves out of trouble suddenly found that they couldn't anymore, and many would have gone bankrupt (and some still did) if their respective governments in many different countries hadn't 'bailed them out' by giving them huge amounts of money. In addition, the government put in place guarantees so that people who lent money or deposited it in a bank could be confident that should the bank be unable to repay, the government would instead. In some of the worst cases, such as with Northern Rock and Royal Bank of Scotland in the UK, the government invested so much money that it became the effective owner of the banks. The combination of these measures, taken in the US, the UK, Europe, and other parts of the world, brought the initial crisis to an end and enabled the global financial system to begin to recover.

This is a brief description of the financial crisis, and it does miss out on a number of significant factors. Some analysis, such as that by members of the US Financial Crisis Inquiry Commission,[88] identify as many as ten different factors acting together, including global, national, individual, historical, and recent components. There's also an excellent documentary, *Inside Job*, by director Charles Ferguson which, whilst focusing on a smaller number of contributing factors, clearly explains the role played by lack of government oversight, a culture of excess in financial services, and the myriad of complicated and confusing financial products.[89] If the outcome of the crisis was simply that banks came close to collapse and then recovered with a large amount of state aid, it would be unlikely that we would still be talking about it quite as much today. Unfortunately, the shock and panic that ensued as the financial services sector stopped performing its key function of lending to businesses and individuals caused the 'real' economy to suffer. Because banks weren't lending, companies that needed to borrow money from banks in the short term to continue to operate found that they couldn't, and many companies went bankrupt. Companies that wanted to borrow for longer-term investments, such as to buy more efficient machinery, couldn't do that either, and so the economy began to stagnate. As businesses went bust or started to think more about short-term survival, many workers were made unemployed. People who would have previously borrowed money to buy a new car or fund home improvement didn't, and instead started to save money to secure their own financial position. Businesses then found that with more people unemployed and more of the employed people saving instead of spending, they were selling fewer goods and services, and making less money. If they couldn't sell their goods and services, then they didn't want to waste money making or supplying them, so they made more of their workers unemployed. As a result of this downward spiral, confidence in the economy quickly slipped away, and fewer companies were willing to invest for the long term or hire more workers. An economic rot quickly set in.

If businesses and individuals aren't earning any money, then they can't pay tax on it. As the economy floundered, the amount of tax that the government was able to collect from businesses and individuals also dropped significantly.[90] This collapse in government income led to a big increase in the national 'deficit', the gap between what the government collects in taxes and what it spends in any given year. The difference between what is spent and what is collected in taxes has to be made up by government borrowing, or debt. Although on the eve of the crisis government debt in the UK was low by historical standards, and around the average of similar developed nations, in the years since the crisis the collapse in government tax revenues has led to a significant increase in government debt (sometimes called 'sovereign' debt).[91] The trend has been seen in most, if not all developed countries, to varying degrees. Yet it was particularly prominent in the UK because financial services make up a much larger proportion of the UK economy than in other comparably sized countries. The disproportionate size of the UK financial service sector is due to the eminence of the City of London as a global financial centre. This not only made UK tax losses proportionally higher, but also greatly increased the cost to the UK of rescuing its banks. The high costs of the financial crisis created an apparent 'sovereign debt crisis'. This is the justification from which the austerity narrative has emerged.

THE AUSTERITY NARRATIVE

THE IDEA OF AUSTERITY stems from the belief that, due to a combination of government incompetence, overspending, and the financial crisis, countries are in too much debt. Following the financial crisis, the difference between what the government spent and what it received in taxes was too great, and this annual deficit has resulted in a large increase in UK sovereign debt. The austerity narrative looks at this feature and proposes that countries are left with just two options. Much like a household that is living beyond its means, they must either spend less or earn more, in order to 'balance the books'. Austerity, or the idea that the government should spend less, is one side of that equation. This logic has led to significant cuts in government spending since the Conservative/Liberal Democrat coalition in the UK won the general election in 2010, and the principles behind it have been accepted even by the opposition Labour Party.[92]

The problem with austerity is encapsulated in the description of the aftermath of the financial crisis provided in the previous chapter. When people think about national austerity measures, they tend to think about them in terms of how debt works for an individual. The logic goes along the lines of this example: if someone earns £1,000 a month but spends £1,500 a month, then they're going to get into lots of debt quite quickly. If they don't bring their spending under control, then they will get more and more into debt and the interest they'll need to pay on that debt will increase. To get out of the mess they are in, that person first needs to stop spending so much. If they are ever going to get their debt back down to a manageable level they'll need to spend a lot less than their £1,000 a month income, so that whatever is left over is not only enough to pay off the interest on their debts each month, but also enough to begin to pay off the amount that has been borrowed. It is this view, scaled up to a national level, which forms the basis of the austerity narrative, and gives the appearance of being a valid response to the sovereign debt crisis.

There are problems, however, with scaling-up this logic to the national level, because a national economy functions very differently to a household budget. The challenge of attributing a feature of a system on one scale to that on another is sometimes described as a 'fallacy of composition'. The government's income comes from taxes it collects from its own people and from the companies that operate within its borders. Its biggest costs (about £300bn in 2013)[93, 94] are for the wages and pensions of the people that it employs, such as teachers, doctors, nurses, police, social workers, and civil servants, as well as things like welfare and unemployment benefits. Most of the people the government employs are being useful; they are providing essential services or helping the country run more smoothly, whether that's teaching children, keeping the roads safe, helping sick people get better quicker, or doing the administration to enable these things to happen. This is of long-term benefit to the whole country, even if it's not always easily financially quantifiable. Government employees are also earning money and spending it in shops and restaurants, and this helps keep the economy ticking over. They are giving money back to the government in the form of taxes, and the money they spend is being taxed at lots of other points in the economy, wherever it ends up. Lastly, these people are not unemployed. They're working and earning, and so are not on benefits or in need of other government financial support services such as housing support. They are being a net contributor, rather than net cost to the country's economy. As well as employing people directly, the government helps boost the economy by investing in essential national infrastructure like road and railways, power generation and distribution, and house building. These projects are essential for the rest of the economy, designated the 'private sector', to run successfully, and they require the creation of jobs for their planning, construction, and maintenance.

When a government tries to save by cutting spending, it inevitably means that less investment is made in the economy, which leads to either fewer people employed, a reduction in wages, or both. To use the previous analogy of the individual, this would be like spending less on travel to get to work, by walking instead of taking the bus, but arriving at work later. The individual would end up spending less, but also earning less as a consequence of those spending choices. On a national level, whether it's directly cutting the number of doctors or teachers, cutting local government budgets that then reduce the level of services, or reducing infrastructure spending that will have employed people indirectly, cuts in government spending ultimately result in workers being paid less, or in there being less work to go around. Scrapping road-building projects means fewer construction workers are needed. Trimming bus routes leads to fewer bus drivers. These redundancies might then trigger further redundancies.

Imagine the government decides to cancel a train-building contract. The train company, having lost the work, decides it needs to cut hundreds of jobs in order to survive. The train company was a major employer in a certain area, and so now in that area there are hundreds more people out of work and not spending as much money. The corner shops, the clothes shops, and the restaurants in that area struggle to make ends meet and so start to close down, laying off their staff, and so on, as the downward spiral continues. All the people that lose their jobs, both as a direct and indirect result of government cuts, are no longer being as productive, spending money, or paying taxes. As they are unemployed, they will also need to take money back from the government in benefits and support services.

This explains why it's so difficult for the government to make cuts. What the government spends makes up such a large part of the economy, (about 42% in 2012-13),[95] that by significantly cutting spending the government is shooting itself in the foot. This approach might reduce some costs, but it increases others such as benefits, and also reduces the government's tax income as the economy grinds to a halt. We can see that while austerity might make sense for an individual in debt, the picture is more complicated for whole countries because cuts lead to higher unemployment, which then reduces tax income and undermines the government's ability to make savings. This is illustrated clearly by both the constraining effect of austerity on the UK's recovery following the elections in 2010, and the link between austerity and growth across the Eurozone economies.[96] There are also a number of other factors that make austerity even less likely to succeed in the long term.

Firstly, as the financial crisis demonstrated, the success of an economy depends largely on confidence. When an economy is growing and everyone is optimistic about the future, they're happy to spend money and make investments, both of which boost the economy further. However when an economy appears to be in trouble and pessimism sets in, people stop spending money and start saving instead because they're afraid of the uncertainty. This lack of spending further restricts economic activity. Additionally in this situation people and companies stop making investments, like launching new products or building new shops and factories, because these already-risky activities are made riskier still by the uncertain economic situation. This then causes further pessimism in a negative feedback loop, known in economics as the 'paradox of thrift'. So confidence of a stable future is absolutely essential to investment. If there's no hope of a positive future then there's no point in companies investing their money, as it's unlikely the future will be stable and benevolent enough for them to make their money back.

Another factor that undermines austerity as a mechanism for widespread recovery is that countries are not independent actors, but interlinked with other countries and regions in complex trading networks. National economies can be boosted or constrained by these connections. If the economies of partner countries are flourishing, then there are lots of people in these countries to buy your country's goods and services, borrow from your country, or lend it money, further boosting your country's economy - and vice versa. When partner countries are struggling, this reduces the market for your country's goods and restricts economic activity. If lots of countries decide to implement austerity measures at the same time, as happened in Europe after the financial crash, then it restrains spending not just at a national but also at an international level, and this further restricts growth in national economies. Countries trying to pay off debt is quite like people standing up in a sports stadium to get a better view; if one person stands up they may gain a clearer view, but if everyone stands up at the same time then standing up does nothing to improve the view at all.

The weakness of the austerity narrative is unfortunately made apparent in almost every quarterly growth report from the economic statistics agencies.[97] Instead of saving the government money, an austerity agenda has led to increased government borrowing, as damage to the UK economy from the cuts outweighs any savings made by the cuts themselves.[98] Government forecasts for economic growth over the last five years have been consistently over-optimistic, with the country spluttering in and out of recession for half a decade after the crisis struck.[99] A genuine, widespread recovery remains a distant dream, with the recent return to GDP growth driven by an increase in population rather than productivity, and the probable inflation of another housing market bubble.[100, 101] Full-time employment is still at worryingly low levels, with many people self-employed, working zero-hour contracts, or part-time on poor wages, only because they cannot find secure, full-time work.[102, 103, 104] This is known as 'underemployment', and it marks a decline in the quality of employment; a nuance that is not reflected in the official employment figures.[105, 106] Wage levels still stand considerably lower than they were before the financial crisis,[107] and the governor of the Bank of England Mark Carney stated upon taking up his role that this is the 'weakest economy in 100 years'.[108]

In the meantime, long-lasting, or 'structural' damage is being done to the economy. In a short recession of six months or a year, those people unemployed during that period can find jobs again once the economy recovers. In a longer recession or period of stagnation, large numbers of people miss out on appropriate work for a long period of time. As a result they can lose skills, fail to keep up with developments in their field, or otherwise become difficult or costly to re-employ as they require re-training. The stresses and strains of living under the pressure of long-term unemployment can create health issues or put increasing pressure on families.[109] Young people that leave school or university struggle to find positions that make the most of, and develop, their skills.[110] They can lose confidence and motivation. Often, the first thing that under-pressure companies or businesses cut are budgets for training or personal development, and if these conditions continue for long periods then businesses can lose their innovative edge. In addition, should the government cut back on investment in key infrastructure such as transport or IT then the long-term potential of the economy can suffer. System breakdowns can become more frequent and more costly, and the failure to maintain or increase capacity can limit the prospects for economic development.

Austerity not only fails to achieve its short-term targets of reducing national debt, but in trying to save money by cutting government spending and allowing the economy to stagnate, it creates huge long-term issues that permanently damage the economy and society, and transfer unquantifiable costs onto future generations. In the meantime, millions of people will experience a far worse quality of life, and endure greater hardship, than they would have done otherwise.

If cutting spending doesn't work though, then what does? We have barely explored the other side of the equation: that of tax rises in order to pay for the deficit. These appear to be so politically unpalatable that they have not really been explored as a solution to the sovereign debt crisis, even taxes on those who are very wealthy. Yet it may be possible to focus taxes on the super-rich and big corporations, who do not spend all their money, and redistribute it to poorer groups, who are far more likely to spend it within the economy. UK corporations are currently sitting on large quantities of money that they are not spending because they have little confidence that those who would purchase their products will have the money to buy them.[111] Taxing those who have spare money sitting around, and distributing it to poorer people who need it, would work to boost the economy and could result in a 'win-win' situation where larger corporations, despite having to pay higher taxes, would be able to make more money because there would be greater demand in the economy for their products.

One historic response however to the kind of crisis we face was put forward in the 1930s in a number of books by the British economist John Maynard Keynes – the key ideas of which came to be known collectively as 'Keynesianism'. He proposed that government spending held the key to escaping from such ruts. He believed that governments should spend less in the good times, but should spend heavily when the economy was in recession, to keep people employed and to get the economy moving again. This was enacted most famously in the USA during the 1930s, where this 'fiscal stimulus' helped bring the US economy out of a deep depression (a particularly severe and long-lasting recession). Similarly, in Europe in the years following World War II, huge increases in spending as a result of the US Marshall Plan of grants to war-ravaged European economies played a major part in helping the countries of Western Europe get back on their feet. The proactive government intervention in economies on both side of the Atlantic until the 1960s is often called the 'Keynesian Consensus'.[112] Following the financial crisis and subsequent global recession, it appeared as if an initial Keynesian response would again be successful. Governments in the USA and the UK borrowed huge amounts of money to spend, and succeeded in stimulating their economies out of the worst depths of the initial crash.[113, 114] By the middle of 2009 both the UK and USA had emerged from the recession and returned to economic growth. However, reductions to spending introduced in the UK in 2010, and the end of major stimulus spending in the USA a year later, put the brakes on the economic recovery, with the UK economy returning to recession.[115] Since then the UK economy has barely grown at all, whilst the US economy has grown slowly and sporadically.[116, 117] Under this austerity, neither economy has come anywhere close to collecting enough taxes and reducing spending enough to reduce overall debt levels.

The austerity narrative in the UK does not appear to be achieving its stated purpose of reducing the deficit, and therefore reducing sovereign debt. The UK government's Office for National Statistics (ONS) shows little change in 2012/13's deficit figures compared to a year earlier, with the government on track to borrow £150bn more by 2015/16 than originally forecast five years before.[118, 119] However, there is also little evidence that the amount of sovereign debt would be much different following a strong economic recovery, however it was to be achieved. This is because the UK national debt is well over £1trillion. Any overall reduction in this figure would first require the elimination of the deficit, which would require the government to increase the tax taken by well over £10bn *a month*, or over 8% of gross expenditure, whilst investing as sparsely in the long-term health of the economy and the country as it is currently. Alternatively, the government could keep taxes at the same level and cut spending by 8%, about the same amount as the entire Defence, Industry, Agriculture, Universities, and Employment budgets combined. To eliminate sovereign debt completely, this favourable period of stable, high growth would need to be sustained for decades, despite the additional austerity or tax rises, and with the government maintaining a large budget surplus (taking more in taxes from the economy than it spent) for that entire period. No government or succession of governments has ever come close to this kind of balance between taxation and spending, even in boom years, and as such there is no precedent for this in the history of our country. No UK government, of any political persuasion, has ever managed to run budget surpluses for more than a few years at a time.

If we look more closely into the economic gloom there are quite a few bits of economic data like this that don't seem to make logical sense. How is it then that, for a country that has almost always run significant budget deficits for decade after decade for the last sixty years, we are not completely bankrupt by now?[120] If our government debt is now over 90% of national GDP and austerity is hurting, how did we recover so strongly following the Second World War when government debt was 240% of GDP?[121] Why, if as a nation we cannot afford our public services, and were forced to cut things like the Educational Maintenance Allowance at £600million a year, (crucial for enabling children from poorer families to stay on in further education), and £11bn worth of benefits and tax credits in 2011, could we afford to provide £375billion worth of investment in the form of 'Quantitative Easing' to the banking sector following the financial crisis?[122, 123] And how is it possible that despite our supposedly terrible financial situation, the government can still borrow money from investors at extremely low interest rates?[124]

It seems that the dominating austerity narrative is not the whole story. Huge national debt, expensive and inefficient services, and unaffordable public spending are part of a tale that, whilst containing elements of truth, does not stand up to scrutiny.[125] The negative cycle that results from austerity measures, as well as the living evidence of our current economic situation, shows that austerity does not offer us a viable way forward. The negative economic messages that the austerity agenda sends about our economy, our ability to afford public services, and the government's capacity to spend, are at odds with the apparent ease with which vast amounts of money were found to bail out the banking system.

Gaining a clear picture of our current economic situation is important if we are ever to find a way back to a healthier economy, let alone overcome the massive environmental challenges we face. Yet awareness of the financial crisis and the flaws in the austerity narrative alone, whilst valuable, don't provide us with solutions. Increased government spending that would break the cycle of austerity and return the economy to widespread growth might provide a start, but does little to solve the environmental questions that continual growth entails. In addition, there are some aspects of the response to the financial and sovereign debt crises that just don't seem to make sense. It is this last point that helps show the way forward.

It is strange that for all the talk of debt and austerity that dominates our political conversation, there is so little direct discussion about the nature of the stuff that drives our whole economy, and by which we measure its success or failure: money. This might be because it is so ubiquitous; everyone knows what money is, don't they? It might also be because there is simply an assumption that money, like water in a bucket, is a useful measure of the economy, but plays very little role in shaping it. However, the concept of money appears to be poorly misunderstood. What it is, and how it is created and distributed in our system, are the biggest determining factors in each of the financial crisis, our current national indebtedness, and our failure to live sustainably within the limits of our environment. As a result, an understanding of what money is and the role it plays will not only show us how we might drag ourselves out of our current predicament, but will give us the framework we need to envisage the stable, sustainable future essential to the continual prosperity of the human race.

MONEY

Every day, billions of people all over the world reach into their pockets, wallets or purses and hand over their money to other people in exchange for food, medicines, haircuts, advice, and countless other goods or services. Almost everyone will do this unthinkingly, without giving a moment's thought as to where that money came from, or why, when it was exchanged for goods or services, the other person agreed to swap it. Money might be everywhere, and we might view it as one of life's constants, but it is not as permanent as we may first believe. There have been different types of money used in different places and at different points throughout history, and we'll look at some of these shortly. As well as this, we'll see that its usefulness and continued value are based on little more than trust.

Money performs three main functions, and understanding this allows us to analyse why complicated societies like ours would have money in the first place. At the simplest level, money allows people to store value, so they don't have to carry less convenient things, (like gold bars, for example), around with them. To be really useful it should also store value over a longer time period than goods that might expire, such as fresh food. Secondly, money is used as a 'medium of exchange' in a bartering or market system. Without money, exchanging goods and services would require either a willingness to exchange things of different values, meaning that one side in the exchange would lose out, or an exact match between what one person wished to sell and another wished to buy. As an example, if someone had firewood that they wanted to exchange for some food, they would have to find someone who specifically needed firewood and also had food available with which to barter directly with. Without money, in a complicated society like ours, many of these wants and product surpluses would remain unmatched, and so goods would be inefficiently distributed. Using money, (with its stored value), someone could sell firewood to anyone who wants it in exchange for money, and then use that money to buy spare food from anyone who has some. Whatever is used for money should thus enable people to buy and sell goods and services more easily.

Finally, money serves as a 'unit of account'. This means it is a convenient way of agreeing how much someone has. Using the above example, if Person A has some firewood and a pig, they might be seen to be as wealthy as Person B, who also has some firewood and a pig. The information missing in that account is that Person A's firewood is made from a soft wood, whereas

Person B's firewood is hardwood and so is of a better quality. Person B's pig is also fatter and tastier than Person A's. It would be challenging to record that accurately for more complex purposes - such as tax - using only descriptive measures (how much fatter? how much tastier?). Recording the information using monetary-exchange value is much easier.

Money has developed over thousands of years in different forms, some of which are quite ingenious and surprising. Some forms of money in use hundreds of years ago we now describe as 'commodity money'. This included things like gold and silver coins. The value of commodity money comes from the rarity and desirability of the commodity or material that it is made out of. When we think of money in historical terms, this is perhaps what comes to mind. Commodity money is not widely used as money in the modern world, and is not a good store of value because the value of the material itself might change depending on its usefulness for other things or how much of it there is. Commodities such as gold, however, are often still attractive for investors or speculators, who purchase them in the hope that their value will increase over time.

The most ancient forms of money that we are aware of were of the 'unit of account' function described above. These were records carved on stone or wood that marked who, within a community, owed what to whom. They were often held by a trusted village leader or religious institution, and were created when people in the community entered into a debt or obligation with each other. When goods or services changed hands these recordings were then changed to reflect the new reality, or destroyed once the debt was repaid. In some cases the records were notches made on wooden 'tally' sticks, which were then split down the middle and kept in two locations so that they couldn't be fraudulently altered. These records are surprisingly similar to the system of money in use today.

The terms 'representative' or 'fiat' money describe the notes and coins in circulation in modern economies across the globe.

Their value does not come from the value of the commodities they are made of which, as small pieces of paper or metal, is negligible. The value of representative money currencies like the GB Pound Sterling and the US Dollar comes from two places. One is its acceptance by the government of the country in which it is used for the payment of taxes. The second is the confidence the public has in accepting it and using it within the economy. The public demands the currency, as wages in return for work, or to pay for food and clothes and haircuts, and so it maintains its value. In addition, the fact that governments don't often suddenly withdraw support for a currency also helps. The public can have confidence that tomorrow, next week, next month, or next year, the money in their wallet will be worth approximately what it is worth today. It is because of this implicit trust in its value that most of us just get on with using money freely, and don't worry about it too much. The ultimate guarantee is the fact that a stable government confirms the value and legitimacy of that money by accepting it back in payment for taxes.

As a result of this, it can be useful for us to think of money not as a commodity with an inherent value, but as a kind of unspoken social contract. If Person A is selling a pig and Person B wants to buy one, Person B trusts that Person A will accept money as payment. At the same time Person A trusts that the money exchanged will be ascribed the same value by the person that they want to buy something else from tomorrow. In turn, that other person trusts that when they put that money in the bank overnight, the bank is going to give them back that money, at the same value, the following day.

It is little more than trust that also gives commodity money its value. A gold or silver coin is worth only as much as its value is trusted by the community of people who use and exchange it. If no-one wanted gold then it wouldn't be valuable. I could have all the gold in the world, but if nobody else wanted it then it would be worthless and I couldn't use it to buy anything.

What's more, even if some people wanted gold but doubted that other people in their community would, then their trust in it as money would be eroded, and its value would drop, maybe even to the point of it being useless as money in that particular community. The same fate could also befall money as a record etched on stone or wood. It is only trust in the accuracy of those records that makes them worth anything. Far from being of permanent value, money can actually be thought of as quite 'fragile'. We can also see that it's possible that a wide range of things could perform the function of money within a community, provided that there is trust in their value.

The different forms of money described above are reflected in the system of money that we have in the UK today. The most obvious form of money that we use is cash: notes and coins. We probably think of these first when we think of money because they have a certain physical permanence, but there are other forms of money in use that are less 'physical', but just as trusted, and far more widely-used. In fact in our system cash makes up less than 3% of the total money in the economy.[126] Cash is money that is created by the Bank of England (known as the UK's 'Central Bank'). This is then lent to commercial banks such as RBS, Barclays, and Lloyds, to put in cash machines and shop tills so that we, the public, can get hold of it and use it for our transactions. However the vast majority of money in the economy, (the other 97%), is known as 'commercial bank money' and, much like the tally sticks mentioned earlier, is nothing more than a digital record of a monetary relationship, stored in computer systems. This 97% of money in existence is created by the commercial banks, (the people that we, the public, bank with), when they give out loans or allow overdrafts.[127] Much like the tally-sticks, it is created upon the agreement of a new debt relationship, and is made by the bank simply typing the numbers into a computer. Let's look at how this works in more detail.

Let us say that Person A walks into a bank and asks to borrow £1,000. After credit checks and other diligence are performed, the loan is agreed. What the bank then does is start an account in the name of Person A, and then create £1,000 in it by typing the numbers into a computer. Person A is then free to spend that money on home improvements, or a car, or anything else that they wish. They can transfer it to a different bank account that they have, transfer it to another person's account, or take it out as cash. It is real money. Following the loan from the bank to Person A, there is £1,000 more in the economy than there was before.

If this all seems incredibly simple and quite unreal to you, then you are not alone. The renowned economist JK Galbraith captured this when he said that 'the process by which banks create money is so simple that the mind is repelled'.[128]

It's hard to imagine that the money circulating around our economy is created so effortlessly, and apparently inconsequentially. It also challenges many popular conceptions of banks. If simply typing on a computer can create money, then what does this mean for the money that we see in our accounts? Don't banks have to have money already before they can lend it to us? The best way to answer these questions is to take a trip back a few hundred years and look at a story about the development of modern banking.

The creation of modern banking

Originally a bank was a safe place where people stored (deposited) their valuables like gold or silver. Many of the first modern bankers were actually goldsmiths, who found that their secure vaults in which they stored their precious crafting materials were in demand for storing other people's valuables too. So let's imagine that Person A deposits ten gold bars at his local Goldsmith. To record the transaction, the Goldsmith gives Person A a receipt. Now the next day, Person A wants to take a gold bar back from the Goldsmith, in order to buy a horse. However, a gold bar is quite heavy to carry around, and so after a brief conversation with the Goldsmith, they agree that the Goldsmith will accept the receipt in return for the Gold regardless of whomever it is that brings it in and makes the claim. In this simple agreement, the receipt has become more than just a receipt: it is a 'promise to pay'. Now Person A can use this to buy his horse from Person B - provided Person B agrees.

Now, there are some potential issues that could arise. Person B could refuse to accept the receipt, or 'promissory note', and instead prefer to stick to cold, hard gold. Alternatively, Person B could accept the promissory note, but when trying to exchange it back into gold at the Goldsmith's, the Goldsmith could refuse. So in order for the promissory note to be accepted both by Person B, and then by the Goldsmith again, there needs to be trust between all parties. In order for that to happen, there probably needs to be a community of some kind so that Person B knows the Goldsmith beforehand, and knows that he is good to his word. In this example we can assume that, because of the convenience of using promissory notes from the Goldsmith instead of carrying gold around, their use was widely accepted in that community. The creation of modern money has begun.

In the next stage, after the use of promissory notes for transactions has become widespread, the Goldsmith has a eureka moment. He realises that Person A probably isn't going to take his gold back out of the bank anytime soon, and even if he did he wouldn't take it all out at once. The Goldsmith therefore decides to lend out some of Person A's gold, (in the form of more promissory notes), to other people, (who need to borrow some gold to make bigger, longer-term investments, like building a house). The Goldsmith has realised that instead of having all that gold, including his own, sitting idle in his vaults, he can lend some out and in the process earn an income on it by charging interest. In the meantime, other Goldsmiths have set up their own gold storage and lending operations, and there is now a healthy supply of Goldsmiths' promissory notes circulating in the community.

So the Goldsmith gives out promissory notes for two gold bars each to Person C and Person D, and a month later they bring back the promissory notes, plus an extra note or gold bar each in interest. The Goldsmith has now acquired more wealth by loaning out someone else's assets - the gold - that he was meant to be looking after. Whilst this initial loan could be a bit risky, as for a while he had issued more promises for gold, (to Person A, Person B, Person C, and Person D), than he had gold in his vaults, it was unlikely that they would all come back at once and demand to exchange the notes back into gold. The convenience of paper promissory notes meant that lots more people decided to give their gold to the Goldsmith for safe keeping in exchange for promissory notes, and as well as this, the initial holders of the notes had spent some of them by buying other things from other people (Persons E, and F). Now a large number of people in the community held the notes, and the likelihood of all of those people all coming into the Goldsmiths at the same time to exchange their notes back into gold was very slim indeed.

The Goldsmith continues for some time lending out gold in the form of promissory notes and earning a handsome profit. Then one day he has an even better idea. He realises that what's important is not that he actually has much gold in store at all (in 'reserve'), but simply that people think he does. All the promissory notes that have been given out so far have been exchanged and widely accepted based upon the trust in his name, and his good word that they can be exchanged back into gold whenever people want to. In the few times that people have wanted to change them back into gold, the Goldsmith has had no trouble performing this transaction. As a result, no one has any reason to doubt that the Goldsmith's promises to pay are worth what he says they are. He realises that he can now create lots of promissory notes whenever he wants and lend them to people, without having to have anywhere near the correlating amount of gold in reserve in his vaults at all. He can charge interest on those promissory notes in exactly the same way as for the gold-backed promissory notes, and earn money from them. As a result, the Goldsmith lends more and more, and becomes very rich. He has become a banker. On the plus side for everyone else, he has also expanded the amount of 'money' circulating around the community, and made it much easier for people to buy and sell things, because it's easier to use paper promissory notes than chunks of gold. As a result the economy of the community is healthy.

Now there are some things that could go wrong for the Goldsmith. Lots of people who borrow promissory notes from him could spend them elsewhere in the community and then go bankrupt, and not be able to pay them back. If this happens the Goldsmith not only loses the potential income from interest charged, but also might lose some genuine gold should those now holding the notes come back and demand to exchange. Even if they don't, by increasing the number of promissory notes circulating in the community, and therefore the 'money supply', the Goldsmith still faces an increased obligation which he will need to be aware of: making sure that he always has enough gold available for people to exchange with promissory notes on a day-to-day basis. If he doesn't then disaster could occur. Word might get around the community that he doesn't have enough actual gold in the vaults to match the obligation of all the promissory notes he has created, and everyone holding the notes might then rush to his door to demand their share of the gold. This is what is known as a 'run on the bank', as happened in 2007 to the UK bank Northern Rock. If there is not enough gold in the vaults to be reconciled with the promissory notes as they are presented then the Goldsmith will go bankrupt.

This illustration goes some way to explain how modern banking works. Commercial banks creating money by typing numbers into a computer is little different to the Goldsmith creating money by writing numbers on a piece of paper and signing it. Perhaps the main difference is that in our system, the scale of the enterprise is an order of magnitude greater. The proportion of commercial bank money (promissory notes) in our system can sometimes outnumber the amount of 'gold' in reserve by as much as 30 to 1. Gold isn't actually used as a reserve any more, but that's another story: one of the best explanations is in the book *Modernising Money* by Andrew Jackson and Ben Dyson.[129] The story of the Goldsmith also highlights why there are some misconceptions about how banking works. A recent survey done by the New Economics Foundation showed that most people believe banking operates either as a 'safe-deposit box', (by holding our money in a vault and then giving it back to us when we ask for it), or by simply acting as an intermediary by taking money from depositors, (who want to bank their money for safe keeping), and lending it out to borrowers, (who might want to buy a car, for example).[130] Both of these views could be seen to originate in the historical allegory of the development of banking described above, but both are now far removed from the reality of banking we have today.[131]

BANKING AND THE ECONOMY

WE HAVE EXPLORED how the vast majority of money in existence today is of the 'promissory note' variety, otherwise known as commercial bank money, which is created when the bank extends a loan or overdraft. It is not backed by any commodity of value, other than the trust that everyone in society places in its role as a means of exchange. It is not a 'cast-iron' concept. It is created and destroyed in huge amounts every day by commercial banks, which are entirely private, profit-driven enterprises.

Furthermore, as the creation of new money into the economy is a fully private transaction between the bank and an individual or company when they request a loan or overdraft, there is nothing particularly regulated about the way that money is created. There are some limits on how much money banks can create, but these are mostly related to the appetite the bank has for taking risks. Because the banks must cover any losses they suffer through created money that is not paid back with their profits, there will be a natural limit on how much money they want to create at any point in time. In reality, though, even this doesn't act as much of a limit, as while lending more adds to the risk that some might not be paid back, it also increases the amount of profit banks can make through charging interest. The most significant limit on the creation of money is the demand for money in the economy: the appetite of businesses and consumers for loans.

In theory then, the supply of money to the economy is a result of demand in the economy for money. As businesses see an opportunity to invest, (in new machinery or goods, for example), and to make money, then they can borrow from the bank - provided they can convince the bank that they can pay it back - and this will result in more money in the economy. Likewise, individuals or households may foresee a period of secure financial income and wish to borrow to go on holiday, buy a new car, or build a house extension. The problem is, however, that the vast majority of all created money goes nowhere near the 'real' economy of businesses and households. Most created money is lent to investment companies or to other financial institutions for market speculation.[132]

As we covered briefly in the prior chapter on the financial crisis, speculation is about taking a financial risk by betting that the value of a certain product increases or decreases over time. Sometimes, such as when directly buying commodities like oil or steel, those speculating will actually own the product that they are speculating on. However, in most cases the speculation will be on a product 'derived' from the initial underlying asset, and these are known as derivatives. Some of the most well-known derivatives, because of the role they played in the financial crisis, are Asset-backed or Mortgage-backed Securities (ABSs), Collateralised Debt Obligations (CDOs), and Credit Default Swaps (CDSs).

ABSs are individual debts that have been packaged together, or 'securitised', which means they are then big enough to be bought and sold by banks, investors, or speculators on the financial markets. Individual debts would be too small, and so would have to be traded in too great a number to serve the purposes of these large companies. The process of securitisation itself has been identified as a major cause of the financial crisis, by reducing the risk of banks making loans. Traditionally, when banks made a loan they were at risk that the person they made the loan to would not be able to meet the repayments or pay the entire loan back. As a result, banks were very wary of whom they lent money to. With securitisation, banks can make a loan, take an up-front payment for it by selling the loan debt to a trader soon after, and so pass the risk of the loan not being repaid onto someone else. In this way, banks make lots of money simply from the quantity of loans they make, rather than the quality. This leads to riskier lending.[133]

ABSs are bundled together into even bigger packages – CDOs – which regularly contain debt of different qualities, and which again can be bought or sold. Lastly, holders of CDOs can insure themselves against potential losses by buying insurance instruments called Credit Default Swaps (CDSs), which also can be bought or sold on a market. The documentary *Inside Job* describes the trading of CDSs as similar to insuring someone else's house, in the hope that something goes wrong so that you receive a pay-out. The documentary also explains how these three derivatives are really just scraping the surface of the bewildering array of products available to be traded, and it's possible to speculate on anything from commodity prices, to exchange rates, and even the weather.

Another form a speculation is through what are known as leveraged buyouts. In our capitalist system, the ownership of companies regularly changes hands as they are bought and sold. It would be easy to think that when this happens, the person or company who wants to buy another company simply transfers money to the current owner, and the company is exchanged. In many cases, however, companies are not bought with existing money, or even with shares in other companies, but with newly created money borrowed from banks. As an example, Company A might want to buy Company B, which has a value of £300m, but Company A might only have £100m in the bank. What it can do in this instance is borrow £200m from a bank or a number of other financial sources, in order to have enough to purchase Company B. The burden for repaying the £200m back to the bank is then transferred to Company B, which is now £200m in debt, simply for having changed owners. This has happened to a number of major UK businesses including rail companies, and such household names as Debenhams, Caffè Nero, and the football club Manchester United.[134] The reason that this is considered to be speculation is because the purchases are often short-term projects. Purchasers aim to make money, not necessarily from running the purchased companies in a sustainable, long-term manner, but simply from the hope that the value of the company might quickly rise so that it can be sold on again for a profit. When leveraged buyouts occur, the bank funding provided to complete the purchase is entirely new commercial bank money, created in exactly the same way as for loans to customers described in the previous chapter. £200m for a leveraged buyout is £200m more money (and so debt) circulating in the economy than there was before.[135]

In 2012 the global annual value of derivative trading alone was over $640 trillion dollars,[136] a figure so vast it's virtually impossible to comprehend. To try and put this into perspective, that's ten times the GDP of the entire globe, which that year stood at $67 trillion. All this money created for the purpose of speculation on property, commodities, derivatives, and other products wildly increases the instability of the global financial system, and this was another factor in the financial crisis. This is because of the way that the amount of money created and circulating in financial products has far outgrown the economic assets that support it. This issue is explained by Ha-Joon Chang:

> '...the point is that the same underlying assets and economic activities were being used again and again to 'derive' new assets... The result was an increasingly tall structure of financial assets teetering on the same foundation of real assets. If you make an existing building taller without widening the base, you increase the chance of it toppling over.' [137]

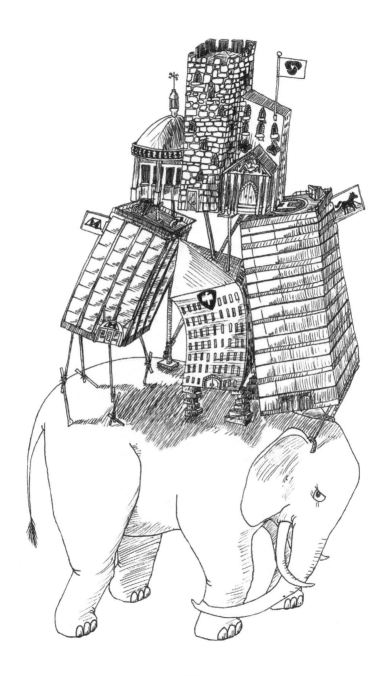

It is important to note that all this extra money typed into existence as the result of the creation and trading of these products has little positive impact on the rest of the economy. It is entirely speculative: it does not lead to more houses being built, or to more factories or greater production. It simply increases profit margins and bonuses in the financial sector. It also increases the prices of goods and services, known as inflation. When money is created to be invested in factories or machinery, then the extra factories and machinery enable more goods to be created in the economy. So although the amount of money in the economy has increased, there is a corresponding increase in the amount of goods and services to purchase with the new money. As a result, prices stay roughly the same. By contrast, lending for the purposes of speculation on the future prices of existing assets, such as houses or company shares, creates more money in the system (more demand) but does nothing to increase the supply of goods or assets.[138] As a result, the only possible outcome is that prices increase, causing inflation.[139] This is a feature of our financial system that we'll look at in more detail later in this book. According to a recent report by management consultancy Bain Capital, global capital tripled between 1990 and 2010, driven by the creation of money for speculative purposes.[140] The inflationary effects of this increase include the tripling of prices for farmland in the last decade and the tripling of UK house prices between 1990 and 2007.[141, 142]

It appears that it is detrimental to arrange our financial system in a way that is largely disconnected from the real economy, and to allow these kinds of financial products to be freely bought and sold in large quantities. Lord Turner, the then Chairman of the UK's Financial Services Authority, went as far as describing the financial services sector in its current form as 'socially useless'.[143]

Trading in derivatives also encompasses speculation on commodities; most disastrously on food. There is now considerable research highlighting how commodity speculation serves to drive up the price of food, causing real poverty and hardship in poorer countries where people can no longer afford the rising prices for key staples such as rice.[144, 145] An in-depth report by Friends of the Earth called *Farming money: how European banks and private finance profit from food speculation and land grabs* explains it clearly:

> *'The huge growth in financial speculation has led to prices no longer being solely driven by supply and demand, but also increasingly by the actions of financial speculators and the performance of their investments. Excessive speculation has forced food prices to rise in recent years and has increased the frequency and scale of price volatility... While high food prices hit the most vulnerable the hardest, threatening their right to food, the rapid price swings also affect poor farmers, threatening farm viability and making it more difficult for farmers to maintain a predictable income'.*[146]

In addition to its role in inflation, the creation of money for speculative purposes also contributes to instability in the financial system, through the creation of market bubbles and by exacerbating the cycle of 'boom and bust'. If the economy grew at a steady rate, people could invest their money with knowledge of a probable return on their investment, and there would be little risk that the economy would suddenly plummet. In reality, the economy has fluctuated between booms, or periods of rapid growth, and busts, where the economy stalls or drops into recession. The way money is created and allocated makes these cycles worse, rather than better. As the economy grows, there is increased confidence, and so greater demand for people wanting to make investments, in order to profit from the growth. Similarly, during these good times banks are more confident in lending, and the combination of increased demand and ready supply creates extra money in the system. The extra money pumps up prices even further, making borrowing for speculation look even more profitable, which creates even more money in the system. Eventually, however, confidence gives way to fear that prices are too high, and that genuine economic activity is not keeping pace, which dissuades investment (as it starts to look too risky) and causes the economy to stall. When this happens, the banks stop creating money through lending, because without growth, there's greater risk that investments will go wrong and people and companies won't be able to pay back what they borrow. As a result, the economy crashes.

To further compound these issues, during economic slumps people tend to save money rather than spend it. This saving pays off debt, and so reduces the amount of money in the economy. We'll look at how this works in more detail in the next chapter. The theory of Keynesianism suggests that it is therefore the government's responsibility to produce economic stability by countering the boom and bust cycles of private bank money creation and speculation. When the economy is growing rapidly, governments should help cool it down by reducing the amount of money in circulation. This is done by increasing taxes and cutting government spending. In turn, Keynesianism proposes that when the economy is stalling, the government should boost it by increasing spending and lowering taxes.

The way that our money system works in the UK creates instability in our financial system and produces economically damaging outcomes. The role of commercial banks in money creation ensures that money is circulated into and around the economy in a way that creates high asset prices, price fluctuations, economic uncertainty, and financial crises. Researchers have identified that there has been a banking crisis in the UK every fifteen years on average since 1945, and *one hundred and forty-seven* worldwide between 1970 and 2011.[147] Furthermore, in our current system money is simply allocated in the economy to wherever it can produce the most individual profit, rather than where it might meet the actual needs of the wider economy or society as a whole. It is this system that led Sir

Mervyn King, the former governor of the Bank of England, to state that: 'of all the many ways of organising banking, the worst is the one we have today'.[148]

PROFITS AND SUBSIDIES

THE UK PUBLIC pays a heavy price for its banking system, in the form of financial instability that undermines the rest of the economy. It also pays as a result of direct and indirect transfers of wealth. Banks extract huge profits from the UK economy by holding a monopoly on money creation, and by benefitting from large subsidies they receive from the rest of society.

Bank profits are so large because of what is known as 'seigniorage': the financial benefit accrued from having the power to create and govern the money supply. They benefit financially from this power because, unlike any other business, what they sell (money) costs them almost nothing to produce. Most other businesses and industries have to buy and maintain goods, which they then sell on, and make careful decisions about what levels of goods to keep in stock. Banks, on the other hand, sell a product that costs them almost nothing to make, as it is created by simply typing into a computer. It's equivalent to running a car hire business that doesn't actually own any cars, but can instantly create a car on demand for free as soon as a request was made to hire one. It would not be inaccurate to think of the entire money supply in the UK economy, (well, 97% of it), as being 'on loan' from private banks.

The banking sector regularly turns out profits of tens of billions of pounds a year. To put that in perspective, the £35bn profits of banks in 2012 were greater than the entire national budget for policing and justice, and only slightly less than the budget for defence. With these profits, banks can do a number of things. Firstly, they can pay them out as bonuses to their staff. We've seen earlier in this book how the incentive structure at banks has been blamed for playing a substantial role in the financial crisis. It did this by encouraging staff to make huge investments and loans in order to earn large bonuses, even if the loans and investments were extremely risky. Despite bankers' bonuses coming under growing criticism since the financial crisis, bonuses paid out by the financial services industry still account for around two-fifths of all bonuses paid in the economy. In 2010/11, bonuses for financial services workers amounted to £14billion, compared to £21billion for the rest of the economy put together.[149]

Secondly, banks can pay out dividends to shareholders with their profits. Across the industry, dividend payments can amount to billions of pounds a year. Thirdly, they can use that profit to boost their capital reserves (the amount of 'money' they actually own themselves, or the amount of 'gold' in the vaults). Keeping their profit as reserves should help banks be more secure, as with more capital they would be able to endure more losses without going bankrupt. Unfortunately, research shows that in the past banks have used higher reserves to make more loans and so higher profit. This means that under the current system, asking banks to keep more capital reserves in order to become 'safer' can actually be counter-productive, leading to them becoming bigger and more risky.[150] The two biggest risks to a bank (as well as almost every other business), are 'liquidity' risk and 'solvency' risk. Liquidity risk describes how a bank might, for various reasons, be unable to pay their bills or meet other payment requirements - not because they don't have enough money, but because they don't have enough money *now*. Brought down to an individual human scale, it would be the equivalent of using all of our money to buy a house but then being taken to court because we didn't have enough left to pay the electricity bill. The problem is not that we don't have enough wealth: it's that we don't have it in a liquid-enough (easily accessible-enough) form at the time when payments need to be made.

Solvency risk, on the other hand, describes how the value of all debts could become greater than the value of all things owned. On an individual scale, solvency risk is tricky to establish because of income and other factors. If I didn't own or earn very much, perhaps living in rented accommodation, but I had a £30,000 credit card debt, then I might struggle to pay off the debt each month, and I might be declared bankrupt, or 'insolvent'. Alternatively, I could be in the same situation but be earning a big salary, so that even though I had the same amount of debt, I could manage the debt-repayments. Banks on the other hand are forbidden under UK law from becoming 'balance sheet insolvent', which means that regardless of their prospective profits, future earnings or any other factor, they are not allowed to continue operating if the value of all that they owe (their debts) exceeds all that they own (their assets).

What we saw in the financial crisis, as described in the prior chapter on that topic, was a failure that was slightly more nuanced. No UK bank initially failed because of insolvency or illiquidity, although some got very close to this; instead the unfolding crisis in the US, UK, and elsewhere shook the confidence that banks had in each other. The fear that other banks *might* become insolvent or not be able to pay back loans meant that banks stopped lending to each other. As banks could no longer borrow from each other, they faced the genuine possibility that they might go bust, at which point the government was forced to step in. The government had little choice in this, as failure to do so could well have led to the complete collapse of the banking system as a whole. If one bank collapsed, then all the other banks that it owed money to might have to write-off that debt, which could have forced some of the other banks to become insolvent, and so-on, until very quickly the system would have failed. Electronic payments and commercial bank money, which we rely on for the vast majority of our economic transactions and which make up the majority of our savings, would have ceased. In addition cash, which only accounts for about 3% of all money in circulation, would have quickly run out – especially as people resorted to hoarding. It's not too much of a stretch to imagine a very rapid and significant breakdown in society. The government had no option but to intervene.

Banks had not only become 'too big to fail', but the system as a whole had become too interconnected and unstable to be allowed to function on its own. As a result the UK government stepped in with a £500bn rescue package – just £100bn less than the entire annual government budget at the time.[151] This money was divided up to perform a number of different roles. About £50bn was used to buy stakes in the banks to provide stability, which led to the UK government owning about 80% of the Royal Bank of Scotland, as well as significant stakes in other banks. The remaining £450bn was set aside for a range of emergency loans and guarantees, in order to return confidence to the system and assist banks in lending to each other again. Despite initial jitters, this massive injection of public money into the financial system, combined with similar interventions in other economic zones such as North America and Europe, helped to return a degree of confidence to the system, at least to put it past the point of immediate danger of collapse.

As a result of this massive intervention, and the deep recession that followed the financial crisis and undermined the UK tax income, public debt leapt up from just over 35% of GDP in 2007/08 to over 60% of GDP in 2010/11, and to 90% by 2013/14. It is still growing rapidly.[152] Despite the large increase, it is still not particularly high by historical standards, and such is the demand from big investors and pension funds for safe places to put their cash, the government can still borrow at very low rates of interest. This sits rather uncomfortably with the austerity agenda that the government regularly tells the country is absolutely necessary. The austerity agenda also sits uncomfortably with the role of the Bank of England in 'quantitative easing', or QE for short.

You might think that the Bank of England should just 'print money' to lend to the government, but under Article 104 of the Maastricht Treaty that governed the creation of the European Union, this is forbidden.[153] In order to borrow money, therefore, the government issues 'bonds' which are effectively a contract or promissory note which is purchased by investors like banks, big companies and pension funds. The government borrows money from investors in exchange for bonds, and then promises to repay the bondholder at a certain rate of interest for a certain period of time. Through the process of quantitative easing, the Bank of England purchased £375bn of government bonds back from banks and elsewhere in the market, (this is in addition to the £500bn government rescue package). This effectively replaced these safe, long-term investments that the banks owned, with Bank of England reserves, (the best and most 'liquid' kind of money). It was hoped that, by propping up banks in this way, they would feel more confident about taking more risks and start to lend again, and so start to increase the amount of money in the economy.

Unfortunately, banks didn't really start lending again for a number of reasons. We won't go into those in detail here, but perhaps the most significant one is that QE only has an indirect effect on money creation by banks. As we've discussed, the biggest factors influencing money creation are the demand for money and the confidence that banks have to lend it, and QE does little to change this.[154] In addition, banks are just as likely to use the central bank reserves they received through QE to speculate on prices, rather than invest and stimulate the real economy. Alternatively, they might use the reserves they received to pay off existing debt, which would actually reduce the amount of money in circulation rather than expand it. As a result, following the first £200bn of quantitative easing, there was a reduction in money creation by banks in 2011, and in 2012, following the next £175bn of QE, the economy moved back into recession.[155]

What QE did achieve however, was that through the Bank of England's purchase of £375m of government debt from investors, the government now owed a large portion of its debt to the Bank of England.[156] Although the Bank of England is independent, and initially said that it would try and sell the bonds back into the market once the economy recovers, they have recently suggested that this is unlikely to ever happen.[157] There will be new government bonds being issued for a long while yet, and so little chance that there will ever be a need to recirculate old ones.[158] The Bank of England, whilst being independent in terms of the decisions it makes within its defined economic role, is in practice owned by the government. So although it may be rarely acknowledged in official circles, by the process of QE the Bank of England has effectively reduced the national debt by £375bn, bringing the total debt back down from 80% of GDP in 2012 to around 60% again, with the 'stroke of a pen.'[159]

This idea is difficult to get our heads around, not least because it seems wrong that such huge amounts of money can apparently be manipulated so easily. However, it's even possible that the £500bn bank bailout intervention by the government could have been set up via the Bank of England instead, so as not to burden the public (via the government) with all the extra debt at all.[160] If banks can be supported by the Bank of England now through QE, then there is no reason it could not have borne the risks associated with the bailout at the time. As Collins et.al put it in Where Does Money Come From?:, 'it would appear that previously unconventional policies... can become conventional if the economic need appears sufficiently pressing.'[161] The case for austerity based on overwhelming levels of public debt stands up neither in a historical context nor a practical one. It is a political decision; there are the financial means and ways to avoid it.[162]

With the role that our current banking system played in the financial crisis, it would make sense if we made the banking sector bear the cost of the massive damage it has caused to our economy, which is thought to amount to at least £1.8 *trillion* but may be as much as £7.4tn in lost output in the UK, or between $60tn and $200tn globally.[163] Yet in a paper for the Bank of International Settlements, Andrew Haldane, the Executive Director for Financial Sustainability at the Bank of England, highlighted how this can never be the case. Our current banking system literally causes more damage that it is worth:

'It is clear that banks would not have deep enough pockets to foot this bill. Assuming that a crisis occurs every 20 years, the *systemic levy needed to recoup these crisis costs would be in excess of $1.5 trillion per year. The total market capitalisation of the largest global banks is currently only around $1.2 trillion. Fully internalising the output costs of financial crises [with a bank levy] would risk putting banks on the same trajectory as the dinosaurs, with the levy playing the role of the meteorite'.*[164]

Instead, we find that the sector has benefited from hundreds of billions of pounds of public money in direct funding and guarantees. Banks know that they will be bailed out and supported should they get into trouble, and so are able to take greater risks and, as a result, make greater profits. This 'too-big-to-fail subsidy' from the public, when added to other subsidies and the value of seignorage, has been calculated at between £30bn and £50bn a year for each of four years prior to 2012.[165] [166] Subsidies of this size comfortably trump the amount that the banking sector returns to the government in the form of taxes and levies, amounting to about £20bn a year in 2012, or just 4% of the national tax take.[167]

THE DEBT IMPERATIVE
FOR GROWTH

IN EARLIER CHAPTERS we looked at our monetary and financial system and examined how money is a public good. Its value derives from the confidence that the public place in it, and the fact that the government accepts it back in taxes. Despite this, it is private banks, rather than the government or anyone else, who through their lending decisions determine the total amount of money in the economy and how it is allocated. As a result, the majority of money is diverted towards unproductive speculation in financial products, which drives up house prices as well as commodities such as food, causing hardship for the poor.[168] Little is invested productively to help the economy grow over the long term.

Furthermore, the way the system is structured makes it inherently unstable, and leads to market bubbles, financial crises, and recessions. Each of these have substantial economic and societal costs in terms of unemployment, reduced tax income for the government, lost economic production, and system bailouts. Despite this, the monopoly that private banks have over money creation, and the fact that creating their 'product' costs them very little, enables them to profit greatly from the rest of society. In addition, banks continue to pay their top employees huge bonuses whilst at the same time receiving subsidies of many tens of billions of pounds a year from the public, by virtue of being 'too big to fail'. Banks are given a privileged position in our society, yet have continually engaged in risky, unfair, and in some cases illegal activity in the pursuit of making even more profit. This has been demonstrated not only by the financial crisis, but by several other scandals and activities: the payment protection insurance scandal;[169] CPP insurance mis-selling;[170] ISA mis-selling;[171] money laundering convictions;[172] tax dodging;[173] and the truly astonishing Libor, Euribor, Forex, and ISDA rate-fixing scandals, which involved almost every major UK bank.[174, 175, 176, 177]

This would suggest there is a case not just for stronger regulation of the banking system, but a complete change in the way that money is created and allocated in our economy. Money is a public good; it exists for the use and benefit of everyone in the country, and it is essential for the functioning of our economy and society. Its value arises from the trust placed in it by the community that uses it, and from the fact that it is legally backed by our democratic government. What's more, the financial crisis has shown that it is ultimately the public, via its elected government, that guarantees the value and safety of money and the financial system, by financially intervening to support it when the banks cannot. It is the public that pays for the risks and costs of the system we have. Without public use, trust, legal backing, and financial guarantee, our money would be worthless. Under these circumstances it makes little sense for the creation, control, and financial benefits of such a public good to remain in private hands.

This point alone should be justification enough to bring the creation of money under public control. Yet there is one more reason why it makes sense to change the way we create money, and this arises because of the environmental pressures that we covered in earlier chapters. In order to live sustainably on this single Earth, we need to reduce our consumption and therefore our production, from which it follows that we cannot keep growing our economy. Yet we briefly covered in an earlier chapter that increasing efficiency leads to a requirement for ever increasing growth. As production processes become ever more efficient, we need fewer resources and fewer people to make the same product for the same price. This is sometimes referred to as the 'productivity trap'. As a consequence of this increasing efficiency, there are two possible options on how to proceed. One is that we make and consume the same number of products but employ fewer and fewer people. This means that improving efficiency leads to growing unemployment and hardship. The other is that we keep the same number of workers, but produce more and more stuff. This is the imperative for growth: we have to grow in order to keep the workforce employed. In the words of the Red Queen in Lewis Carroll's *Through the Looking Glass*: 'Now, here, you see, it takes all the running you can do, to keep in the same place'.

Yet the efficiency challenge is not the only imperative for growth that we face. The way our banking system works, and the way our money is created by private banks in the form of making loans, or 'extending credit', establishes another imperative. When banks create loans, the act of making the loan creates not only extra money in the economy, but also a matching amount of debt. This is because although the borrower has been given new money to spend, they also have to pay back that same amount. Furthermore, the loan is not extended for free, but rather with the requirement that the loan must be repaid along with a certain amount of extra money we call 'interest'. The growth imperative comes from the fact that when the loan is made, money is created to pay back the initial debt, but not the interest as well.

Let's look at an example. Imagine that Person A goes to their bank and asks to borrow £10,000 to buy a car. The bank agrees, and deposits £10,000 in Person A's account with the bank. They do this by typing £10,000 into a computer, which as we know creates £10,000 out of nothing. What has happened is that £10,000 of money has been created in the economy, and the numbers in Person A's bank account, which are able to be used as money, communicate that the bank has given this money to Person A. However, the other side of the equation is that at some point Person A must pay this money back, so he owes this money back to the bank; Person A is 'in debt' to the bank.

As a result of Person A borrowing the money, not only has £10,000 of brand new money been created in the economy, but also a corresponding £10,000 of debt. This isn't the whole story, however, because in this example Person A must pay interest on this loan of £1,000 (over the term of the loan). But where does this money come from to pay the interest? It is not created when the loan is extended. So we can see that while only £10,000 of money is created, there is now £11,000 of debt in the economy. Or to put it another way, more debt has been created than the money that is required to pay it off. The money to pay off the excess debt must come from elsewhere in the economy. As we have found out, however, almost all the money in our economy is created in this way through banks extending loans. So the money to pay off the interest must come from someone else's loan, which in turn is paid off using the money created by someone else's loan, and so on. It is apparent that in our monetary system, the only way our economy is able to pay off all the debt at the point that it requires repayment is if more money is created by people and companies in the economy taking out more loans, creating an ever-widening cycle of debt.[178]

The growth imperative comes from the fact that if we were to just create more loans and more debt, but keep the economy the same size (by not producing and consuming any more stuff), then there would be more and more money in the system but only the same amount of goods or resources to buy with it. As a result, prices for goods and services would rise, and we'd suffer rapid inflation. By growing the economy, however, and so by increasing the amount of stuff that we produce and consume, we ensure that the increase in money in the system is more closely matched by a corresponding increase in the amount of stuff to buy. This helps keep inflation low and prices relatively stable.[179]

With our financial system as it is, trying to reduce the amount of debt in society does not make our country wealthier as a whole. Almost the exact opposite is true. Paying off our debts reduces the amount of money in circulation in the economy. This is because the process of paying the money back to whichever bank lent it 'cancels out' the debt owed. It not only removes the debt (what the borrower owed to the bank), but also removes the money created (what the bank lent to the borrower). In our current financial system (and please excuse the pun), money and debt are two sides of the same coin. Therefore, reducing the amount of debt in the economy by paying off loans reduces the amount of money for investment, for wages, and for other things that the economy needs in order to grow. In addition, because the process of creating money in the economy creates more debt than the money to pay it back (the interest element of a loan), the act of paying off a debt only removes the initial part of the debt from the economy. The interest debt remains, albeit now somewhere else in the economy. This interest debt can only ever be destroyed by borrowers going bankrupt or otherwise defaulting on their loans. If this happens then the bank has no choice but to cancel (or 'write-off') the money it would have earned from the borrower paying interest, as well as any of the initial borrowed amount still outstanding.

This shows how important it is, from the point of view of the wider economy, that people sometimes default on their loans or that companies sometimes go bankrupt. It forces the banks to write off the created interest debt, but leaves the borrowed money circulating somewhere in the economy. This helps keep the amount of debt in the economy under control. If too much interest debt is created and is allowed to continue to build out of proportion with the amount of stuff produced, or is not kept under check by frequent defaults, then at some point there will be a big readjustment where lots of big defaults happen all at once. This is what happens when financial bubbles burst, and which may sometimes be so big and have such an impact on other areas of an economy that we call it a 'financial crisis'.

So our current financial system requires stable economic growth in order to keep prices under control, and to maintain long-term investment in the economy. Yet in practice a growing economy encourages overconfidence and excessive lending, which creates an excess of money and debt in the system. Because the amount of money in the system increases faster than the size of the underlying economic activity, it drives up prices and creates a financial bubble. When this lack of genuine economic activity becomes apparent through investment failures or defaults, the loss of confidence in the economy reduces further borrowing, and causes other people in the economy to start to pay off existing debt. This in turn reduces the amount of money in the economic system. Banks that previously lent willingly will stop lending into the system to keep the cycle of debt ticking over, and further bankruptcies and defaults occur. Depending on its size, as well as other factors, the bursting bubble may lead to a full-blown financial crisis. In the process companies will have gone bankrupt, loans will have to be written off, and so some of the excess interest-debt will be destroyed. In worst-case scenarios banks will fail and will require bailing out. As mentioned earlier, under our financial system this economic 'readjustment' is essential if the economy is to recover, but it leaves a trail of unemployment, lost wages, and genuine hardship. Financial crises, therefore, are far from an anomaly, but rather an unavoidable part of our 'debt-as-money' financial system. This is reflected in the fact that, despite financial crises seeming like a rare event, there have been twelve in the UK in the last two hundred years, including four in the last sixty years.[180] Just because these crises are unavoidable does not mean they are desirable, and they incriminate the financial system that requires them.

The way the system is designed ensures that the economy is always shackled with debt, requires constant, unsustainable growth and guarantees instability and devastating fluctuations between 'boom' and 'bust'. Yet it doesn't have to be this way. The hundreds of billions of pounds found to bail out the system during the financial crisis, as well as the £375bn injected into the banking system by the Bank of England through the process of Quantitative Easing show that the government can intervene in the system provided there is the political will to do so. What's more, historical examples from our own country as well as others prove that there are many more options open to governments to intervene in the money-creation process, even within the current legislative boundaries, than have been used recently.[181, 182] Beyond the current legislative framework there are further options; even a system this big and far-reaching can be changed. It is a created system like any other, which has grown out of public endeavour, government legislation, and historical convenience. As a result, it can be moulded to serve rather than oppress us. But how do we know what kind of system we should move to?

It's a natural response to feel inadequate for this task. Surely the average person with no specialist knowledge is not allowed to understand or design a financial system? We probably shouldn't expect to be able to define the finer details without reading a book or two and doing a little bit of extra study. Yet a number of practical proposals that explain how the system could be reformed suggest that the banking system should work in the way most people intuitively think that money and banking should work. Rather than money coming into being as a 'debt' to a private bank, money is created as a 'positive', debt-free commodity by an independent public body that decides how much money there should be in the economy. Banks, rather than making profit from speculation and risky loans, would instead make their money the way most people intuitively think banks should work: by taking deposits from savers and lending it out to borrowers.

One of the more comprehensive proposals is that put forward by the banking reform campaign group Positive Money.[183] Under the Positive Money proposals, the money in our bank accounts would be electronic money effectively held either at the Bank of England or with our own banks. Customers could choose whether to keep their money in risk-free 'Transaction' accounts, which would be held securely with the Bank of England, or in interest-paying 'Investment' accounts at their own bank, where it would be invested as they determined, with the risk of any investments to be shared with their bank. The banks would not be able to create money in the economy by lending out money that they didn't have, and instead would make money by taking these deposits from savers and lending them out to borrowers. Any money placed in an investment account would therefore be placed for a pre-agreed length of time and rate of interest, to allow the bank to make secure lending decisions.

Under these proposals, the Bank of England would take over responsibility for injecting new money into the economy on a monthly basis. The decision on how much should be added each month would sit with an independent Money Creation Committee (MCC), free from the control of government or commercial banks, in order to avoid any conflict of interest or abuse of power. Money would be added into the economy at the rates required to ensure economic stability, by giving it to the government to spend into the economy according to its priorities. As this money would not need to be paid back, it would be debt-free money, and could be used to lower taxes, increase employment, pay off national debt, or be given as a 'dividend' to ordinary citizens.

It's quite difficult to grasp just how significant and beneficial these simple changes could be to our economy and society. Firstly, the new system would provide greater economic stability, by eliminating the feedback effect between confidence and money creation that leads to boom and bust. As money creation would no longer tied to the demands for loans, there would be little chance of excess lending and price bubbles, and so little chance of financial crashes. By contrast, the MCC could make decisions to limit the amount of new money created during times of higher economic confidence, and increase the amount during downturns, providing a far more stable economic environment.

In addition, under the new system commercial banks would only lend out money in proportion to the amount invested with them. As this invested money comes with known time-scales and interest rates, it would be much easier for banks to predict how much money they will need and when, and so how much they can afford to lend. They will also be aware of when they are likely to have shortfalls, and so can decide to reduce their lending or borrow from other banks for a short while, in order to best manage their cash flow. The new lending certainty would greatly reduce the risk of a bank failing; this, combined with greater economic stability, would reduce the risk of failure in the system as a whole. Because banks will have a much better grasp of their financial situation, it will be clear much sooner whether they are in trouble, and so in the unlikely event of a bank failing, most investors will get most of their money back. Those individuals who have 'transaction accounts' held at the Bank of England, and choose not to take any risk with their money, will lose nothing.

Secondly, as bank failure would not provide a systemic risk to day-to-day transactions, and the only losses would be relatively small amounts by those who had taken investment decisions (with the full knowledge at the beginning that these entailed a level of risk), all banks, including the biggest ones, would be allowed to fail. Neither the government, nor the Bank of England, nor ordinary citizens would ever again have to bail out an individual bank or the financial system as a whole, nor bear any hidden cost associated with the risk of bank failure. As a result there would be no need for deposit guarantees, too-big-to-fail subsidies, quantitative easing, emergency loans, bailouts, or any other subsidies for the banking system, saving the country tens of billions of pounds every year.

Thirdly, as banks would no longer create money in the system, and would be allowed to fail, regulators would be able to permit the creation of many more banks. As banking would become about taking deposits from savers and making loans to borrowers, the banks that would succeed would be those that best knew their customers, and had best assessed their ability to repay. Bigger banks would not necessarily have an advantage over smaller banks, and there would be genuine banking competition rather than collusion. It would be possible for much smaller banks to exist, with more banks embedded in the life of local areas and communities. This would help make communities more resilient to economic or social challenges. In addition, as banks would have to compete for deposits from customers in order to make loans, they would have to listen far more keenly to their depositors when designing savings products. This would lead to what Positive Money calls the 'democratisation of finance':

'If an individual wants to invest their money (i.e. to lend it to someone else) then they will have the choice, in very broad terms, over where their money is invested. For example, customers may be offered an Investment Account that directs funds to small and medium businesses, or to renewable energy, or to mortgages, etc. The effect is to democratise finance, so that the banks' investment and lending decisions start to reflect the priorities of their customers and as a result society in general.'[184]

Finally, as new money is created 'debt-free' in the economy by the Bank of England and the MCC, there would no longer be a debt imperative for growth. The new debt-free money created would slowly pay off existing debt in the economy, reducing overall debt levels and eliminating the need for the continuous re-issue of new debt, along with the associated expansion in economic production and consumption that is required under the current system. As a result, this system would be compatible with the environmental requirement to reduce overall consumption levels, as the MCC would be able to ensure that there was the right amount of money in the economy to correlate to the reduction in available goods, helping maintain stable prices.

These changes could enable us to have a financial system which helps stabilise, rather than de-stabilise the economy; one that reduces the burden of debt, and that allows banks to fail, holding them responsible for the risks that they take.[185] The changes could be implemented unilaterally, without the need to first secure international cooperation, and would allow for financial services that serve the needs and priorities of wider society, rather than the other way around. Positive Money has produced the legislation necessary for changes to the financial system to occur as soon as the political decision is taken.[186] In addition to the Positive Money proposals, there is a proposal known as the 'Chicago Plan'. Put forward in the USA following the Great Depression of the 1930s, and revisited recently by the International Monetary Fund (IMF),[187] it is something of a middle ground, and would go a long way to stabilise the economic system and reduce the risks of boom and bust without actually moving the creation of money out of private control.

But if changes to our banking system are possible and have such positive benefits, then why does it remain unreformed? This is likely to be due to a number of factors. Firstly, although problems with the existing financial system have been identified for a hundred years or more, whilst people are still experiencing what they believe to be the 'good times', it's very hard to make a case for change. Secondly, until recently there was limited awareness of environmental pressures, and the connection between them and our economic system. As environmental issues become more apparent, it is quite possible that the pressure for financial reform will increase. Perhaps the biggest obstacle to change, however, and the reason why change hasn't yet happened, is the power of vested interests. There are very wealthy, and therefore powerful, interests that have benefited from the banking system being run as it is. Many of these people continue to occupy positions of power in politics and society, and seek to maintain the status quo through their connections and lobbying processes.[188] Many others exercise power less directly, through funding political parties or 'independent' think tanks.[189] The Bureau of Investigative Journalism found that in 2010 the financial services sector made up over half of the total value of donations to the Conservative Party.[190] In a 1924 speech Reginald McKenna, then Chairman of Midland Bank, and former Chancellor of the Exchequer, said:

'I am afraid the ordinary citizen will not like to be told that the banks can and do create money. And they who control the credit of the nation direct the policy of Governments and hold in the hollow of their hand the destiny of the people'.

If our financial system is to change then the power of vested interests will need to be overcome. It will not be easy, but neither is it inconceivable. As we begin to think about the kind of world we want to live in, we need not be constrained by austerity, sovereign debt, or even our financial system. Rather than being a slave to the financial markets, in which a tiny percentage of the population take part, our economic and financial systems can be shaped to serve the needs and desires of a much broader section of humanity. The government does not have to 'get out of the way' of the financial system in order for it to function properly. The system is inherently unstable and continues to rely on government involvement to assure its safety. The system does not allocate the money it creates productively, but instead uses it to inflate the prices of existing assets and commodities. Far from being a drain on the private sector, we can see that there is little reason why the government cannot allocate money more productively than the banks and private sector can.[191] It can do this by investing wisely in the real economy, rather than in speculation, and for the long-term benefit of the majority rather than short-term profits of a few.

What this means is that, when deciding what kind of future we want to plan for, it is not just possible, but practical for us to 'think outside the box' of the existing financial system and the restraints it appears to impose. We can offer an alternative response to the environmental crisis than simply 'more of the same'. We can't conjure up another Earth, but we can have the full, unrestrained use of our ingenuity and financial systems to help us live sustainably within the limits of the one that we do have, if only we have the political will to choose this way forward.

AN UNEQUAL EARTH

OUR ECONOMIC SYSTEM needs to change. Our quest to live within the limits of the Earth's natural capacity to sustain life is at odds with the system of continual growth that our economy prescribes. We must modify our systems to reflect the values that are essential for the future success of the human race.

The key word to describe the required changes is 'limits'. As we explored in earlier chapters, we have one Earth on which to live, not five, and if we are to survive we must learn to live in tune with that reality. This will be a huge challenge on its own, but will be made impossible if we expect that this can be achieved under the current distribution of wealth and consumption in our world, as well as in our individual society. We cannot ask or expect those on our Earth with the least to make do with even less; many of these people need to be allowed to consume more. Likewise in our own country, we cannot ask those with the least to reduce their impact the most; not only is it grossly unjust but almost certainly a mathematical impossibility. The only way we can live within the required limits as a society is if those who currently consume the most reduce their consumption the most, and so on. This is not about targeting some kind of absolute equality; it is the physical reality of living together on a finite planet. If, as the size of the cake shrinks, those with the largest slice want to keep their portion of the cake, then the size of the smallest portions will shrink to a level that can no longer sustain those that have to live on them. The Earth produces enough for us all to survive, but only if those who currently vastly over-consume bring their consumption much closer to the required global average.

It would be very easy if everyone in the world decided that this was necessary, inherently understood the implications, and so reduced their consumption accordingly. This would require a kind of universal selflessness: to deliberately limit what we consume now in order to allow other people to consume more, or to allow other people to consume in the future. While this is something that humans occasionally demonstrate they are capable of, the extent to which this already occurs or may occur in the future is a drop in the ocean compared to what is required. This is not necessarily about widespread selfishness; it could be that people logically recognise that if they make decisions in isolation then they might leave themselves in a vulnerable position. What is needed is collective action, and governments are best placed to take it on the public's behalf through taxation, spending, regulation, and other forms of intervention.

Some people may immediately baulk at this idea. It has become fashionable to talk only in terms of private goods, and completely ignore the benefit of what is common, or 'public'. The loudest 'private sector good, public sector bad!' chants are those of the neoliberal evangelists. Yet we cannot ignore the fact that we are all connected, whether we like it or not. We might still think of ourselves as cowboys all alone against the elements, but we are astronauts, and we can no longer pretend that our laying claim to a share of the Earth's resources has no consequences for other people. We can clarify this further by looking at the concept of 'freedom', which is often touted by those who oppose the government making big decisions on our collective behalf. Their argument assumes that freedom is a universally-understood idea, and that it is always 'good'. The reality is far more complicated.

If we see freedom as the permission for absolute individual choice and autonomy, then everyone may do exactly as they wish. We would remove any kind of control, especially the regulations of government, and it doesn't take a philosopher to see that without government or other kind of political authority there would be no enforceable law, security, or collective rule-base. Complete 'freedom' from government or a similar collective body would actually be terrifying.

If we're uncomfortable with taking the idea of freedom that far then we could try and apply it on a purely economic basis. We could remove governmental support of any kind and people could choose everything through a fair-functioning market - assuming of course that 'fair-functioning markets' would exist without government regulations like property rights, company incorporation, and rules against fraud. This might work well for a time for those who were already in a good economic position, but it would only take people losing their jobs and their incomes for them to see fairly quickly that freedom, without any kind of economic stake, really isn't freedom at all. We can't choose to do what we want if we don't have the economic basis to acquire that from the system. People might fall into debt and because, in the name of freedom, there wouldn't be any government regulation, there wouldn't be bankruptcy laws either; it's likely that we would witness the irony of economic 'freedom' leading directly to debt slavery. In addition, how many of us would genuinely like to see the removal of regulation governing child labour, or bribery: the term we give to buying the services of state employees or representatives in a free market.

So the idea of freedom as complete individual autonomy doesn't pan out quite as ideally as it sounds. Not only does it not work systemically, but not everyone can act exactly as they wish, because some people's desires would clash with the desires of others. Two or more people may wish to make use of the same bit of land or other resource. This can be neatly summed up in the 19th century American phrase: 'Your freedom to swing your fist ends where my nose begins'.[192] Individual freedom can never be absolute. We live in a world, country, neighbourhood or family with other people. We regularly make choices that have an impact on others that might be far beyond our comprehension, and we have to regularly live with the consequences of the choices and decisions of others. We are free to make decisions, but we are not free from the consequences of those decisions. This places limits on what we can do as individuals. Similarly, whilst we are free to do lots of different things, we also have to live within the physical limits of the world around us; this extends from our own physical capacity (everyone is free to run the hundred metres as fast as they can, but no one is free to run it in under nine seconds), to the limits of the Earth, such as when and how much it rains, or how much land there is.

We also have to be prepared to admit that we are not even always free to make our own considered decisions. After all, advertising only works, and money is only spent on it, because it does actually influence how we choose to spend our money. We might wish to therefore avoid advertising, but we are all bombarded with advertising in lots of different forms every day. If we were truly to decide to be free from advertising, then we would live a very strange and isolated existence. We can also never be free from the influence of our parents or communities, how we were brought up, or other experiences that we may have had before we were old enough to live independently; nor from the influence that these factors have had, and will have, on the rest of our lives.

Freedom is a complicated concept. We are free in many ways, but in lots of other ways we are not, and never can be. Perhaps the conclusion to draw is that, contrary to what we may sometimes think we would want, we live life within limits in so many ways. The very nature of being human and living in contact with other people means that freedom can never be about complete autonomy. We are social animals in a social world, and the freedom that we experience is that which we exercise within the system formed by the political, economic, and societal frameworks that we collectively negotiate and agree.

So the concept of freedom does not prevent us from choosing to distribute resources in a way that enables us collectively to live within the sustainable limits of the Earth. Within any society there needs to be a boundary between what are collective resources and those resources which people are allowed to exert control over, which we identify as private property. Yet this boundary between the public and private is not fixed, or even easily defined. It frequently adjusts as taxes change or as laws and regulations are added or removed, depending on the perceived needs of the community or society as a whole. The ingenuity, drive, and risk taking of individuals – so valued and lauded by the private sector – benefits the public through the creative provision of an eye-watering variety of goods and services, which could not be provided through some kind of centrally-organised production. The private could not thrive, however, without the public provision of many things: security and order; roads; bridges; lighting; energy coordination; investment in open-ended research; a safety-net of support for the unemployed or infirm; and regulations such as limited liability for corporations and bankruptcy laws, which allow for and encourage the risk-taking so treasured by the private sector. The two work in a virtuous circle: well-designed public regulation, taxation, and spending should allow private enterprise and energy to flourish in a way that enriches the collective whole.[193]

Despite this mutual benefit, there is a worrying trend within our society to diminish and undermine the public good at every opportunity. This neoliberal ideology has been exalted for decades, and most famously by former Prime Minister Margaret Thatcher, who declared that 'there is no such thing as society'. Over the last thirty years public ownership of important goods and services has been undermined, with the privatisation of key services such as the railways, energy, post and telecoms providers. In addition, elements of stillpublicly-owned services such as the National Health Service, probation services, HM

Revenue and Customs (HMRC) and universities have been moved into the private sector. This has been done despite the services being run efficiently and effectively in their previous form, and in the absence of supporting evidence that private ownership will bring an improvement.[194,195,196,197,198,199] Elderly care has also gone in this direction, with underwhelming, even worrying results, and the trend from policy announcements indicate the government's intentions to privatise a range of other local services, often under strange circumstances.[200, 201, 202] As a bizarre additional feature, many of these public services are 'privatised' by selling them to companies that are often owned by foreign governments. As John Harris writes in the *Guardian*, our government's particular application of neoliberalism seems to be that 'State ownership is obviously fine, so long as it's someone else's State that's doing it'.[203]

George Monbiot expands on the inconsistencies of this trend:

'There is a sacred line that divides the world into public and private property. The line is arbitrary and moves every year: ever further across the public realm. But it is policed religiously. As soon as you can bundle the public wealth you've snatched over the line and into the hallowed ground of the private sector, you can claim sanctuary. ...When the threshold is crossed, everything changes. Money spent in the private sector is deemed by politicians and the media to be a good thing. Money spent in the public sector is deemed a bad thing, even though (or perhaps because) it is more effective at distributing wealth. If you are on the right side of the line, the government will deregulate your business. If you are on the wrong side of the line (schools and hospitals for example), it will subject you to ever more draconian regulation, with cruel and unusual punishments for the slightest resistance to its crazy targets and intrusive inspections'.[204]

The biggest beneficiaries of this privatisation are the consultants and the shareholders of big private companies and the wealthy individuals who run them, who get richer still by capturing this public wealth for their own private gain.[205, 206, 207] By claiming more and more resources for private use, the process concentrates ever more wealth and power into the hands of an already extremely wealthy minority, exaggerating inequality. The level of inequality is staggering and, as Monbiot hints, there is no natural law that pre-destines it. The 'sacred line' between the public and private is arbitrary: it is as it is because the system has been designed that way, often by the people who are most set to benefit from its existence.

It is difficult to get our heads around the extent of inequality that we face in this country alone, never mind across the world. Coupled with the privatisation agenda, the last thirty years have seen a huge upward shift in wealth.[208] While over the last ten years the poorest in society have seen a fall in their real incomes, the wealthiest have seen their incomes increase substantially.[209, 210] The richest five families in the UK own the same amount of wealth as the poorest 20% of the entire population, with the top 1% of the population owning the same wealth as the bottom 55% together.[211, 212] The entire bottom half own less than 15% of total national wealth.[213] This vast inequality is caused, amongst other things, by a flawed tax system that, through regressive taxes such as VAT and loopholes that can be exploited by the wealthy, makes the poor pay a much greater proportion of their income as tax than it does the rich (46% against 34%).[214] The picture is much the same at a local level: in the case of London, the richest 10% of Londoners own over *two-hundred and seventy* times the wealth of the poorest 10%. Britain is now one of the most unequal countries in the developed world.[215]

Across the world as a whole the picture is just as unbelievable. An Oxfam report found that the richest eighty-five people in the world alone own the same wealth as the poorest *half* of the global population of three-and-a-half *billion* people.[216] The top 1% owns *sixty-five* times as much as the poorest 50% put together. Some argue that inequality isn't a problem because anyone can become rich, and there's nothing stopping people working their way to the top; this is the basis of the 'American Dream'. However, not only does this view ignore that the wider the gap between the poor and rich the harder it is to climb from one to the other, it also ignores the systemic bias towards the rich that makes this transition even less likely. Even if it were the case that those from the very bottom could frequently climb the ladder, to paraphrase the Marxist philosopher Herbert Marcuse, a system that allows slaves to become masters and masters to become slaves doesn't change the fact that there are masters and there are slaves.[217] Sometimes the plain figures are hard to comprehend, and a story is required. One such story can be found in reporter Nick Shaxon's recent investigation, published in *Vanity Fair* magazine, into the owners and occupants of the central London residential development 'One Hyde Park'.[218] The level of wealth of some residents, and the level of their expendable income, was highlighted by the fact that some flats in the building were changing hands for £140million, or almost £12,000 per square foot: an area of property the size of a table mat. These super-rich have become so by being in the right place, at the right time, with the right amount of power and ingenuity to capture huge amounts of profit as commodity booms occur (the speculative changes in prices, described in earlier chapters), or when public wealth is smuggled over the line into the 'private sector' as the result of political changes. Perhaps the most famous of these changes was in Russia at the turn of the millennium, which created the 'Oligarchs' like the billionaire owner of Chelsea Football Club, Roman Abramovic. Their wealth is then funnelled through secrecy jurisdictions (also known as tax havens) such as the Cayman Islands or Switzerland, in order to ensure that no or little tax is ever paid on it. Interviewing one such member of the 'super-rich' club, Nick Shaxson discovered the extent to which vast wealth can lead to a disconnection from the reality experienced by the majority of humanity. As he writes:

'Arkady Gaydamak, a Russian-Israeli oilman and financier, explained his elite view of accumulating wealth to me in 2005. "With all the regulations, the taxation, the legislation about working conditions, there is no way to make money," he said. "It is only in countries like Russia, during the period of redistribution of wealth—and it is not yet finished—when you can get a result. How can you make $50 million in France today? How?"' [219]

That it could be considered by anyone that the minimum definitive quantity required to 'make money' is $50million is staggering, especially considering what we know about the Earth's resource limits that we talked about in earlier chapters. If everyone in the world today wanted to live how people in the United States do, we would need five Earths' worth of resources to sustainably accommodate them. Yet the net worth of the 'average' American is just $130,000.[220] If everyone in the world was to be able to 'make money' and spend it the way Arkady Gaydamak proposes to, then we would need somewhere around *one-thousand nine-hundred* Earths to sustain us. The Earth, rather than containing the seven billion people it currently does, would only be able to sustain a population of less than four million, the same number of people that live in Los Angeles. When you look at it like that, there is something not just disconnected, but quite obscene that an individual person could own and consume even $50million worth of stuff, never mind the billions of dollars that a growing number do. If we all wanted to live with the wealth of the world's 1,400 billionaires, as identified by *Forbes* Magazine, we'd need *one hundred and forty-five thousand* Earths to keep us all going – levels of excess that are truly incomprehensible.[221] If, as the famous British naturalist David Attenborough put it, humanity in its current economic configuration is a 'plague' on the Earth, then this kind of concentrated wealth is surely the face-eating zombie viruses of horror movies.[222] Perhaps it's fortunate then that wealth of that magnitude is simply too vast to ever be spent entirely on consumables, even in the world of private jumbo-jets, and that it is simply the way the super-wealthy 'keep the score'.[223]

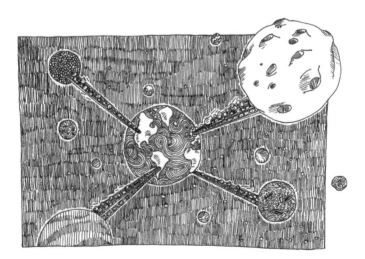

CONTROLLING THE SYSTEM

THE INEQUALITY OF WEALTH in our world occurs because the system is designed to facilitate it: either through the direct planning and implementing of those in power, or their wilful neglect to change the system when its true nature becomes apparent. One way that this is done is through the development, and the permission for the continued existence of, the world's secrecy jurisdictions. Secrecy jurisdictions, sometimes called 'tax havens', create regulation that provides a legally-backed veil of secrecy, so that people who don't actually live there can avoid the rule of law in their own country. This is most commonly used for the avoidance or evasion of taxes, but also for criminal acts like money laundering or the corruption of public servants.[224] When people think of tax havens they often think of palm-fringed islands and, while this is true to an extent, major secrecy jurisdictions also include Switzerland, Luxembourg, and the USA.

A special place in the world of tax havens though goes to our own country, Britain, for its position in the centre of a web of what are effectively UK-controlled secrecy jurisdictions such as Jersey, Bermuda, the British Virgin Islands (BVI), and the Cayman Islands.[225] Nick Shaxson's book, Treasure Islands: tax havens and the men who stole the world, explains how at the centre of the web lies the City of London, a remnant of Britain's colonial past and a 'state within a state', whose army of bankers, lawyers, accountants, and 'tax planners' work to hide the true

117

financial position of Britain's, (and the rest of the world's), richest individuals and companies.[226, 227] The work of the City enables the wealthy to avoid having to pay what they should in taxes to society for the services that society provides in return.[228, 229] This is a service that the less wealthy cannot afford to procure, and it is they that have to pick up the bill by meeting the country's shortfall in tax revenue that inevitably ensues. Attempts to crack down on tax cheats in the UK are compounded by substantial government cuts to the tax investigating and collecting body HM Revenue and Customs (HMRC), and by failure within HMRC to tackle tax avoidance in large companies – the area with the greatest amount of uncollected tax.[230, 231, 232, 233] Official HMRC figures put the amount of tax avoided or evaded, known as the 'tax gap', at £35billion a year, but this figure is described as just 'the tip of the iceberg' by Parliament's Public Accounts Committee.[234] Some experts put the true amount of tax lost at over £100billion annually.[235] This is a large enough sum to counter all the government's austerity measures, increase employment, provide much-needed new investment, and still have plenty left over.[236, 237]

If the consequences of tax havens are bad for Britain then they are truly devastating for developing countries. Some of the poorest countries in the world have vast proportions of their national product stolen through 'illicit outflows' by corporations or wealthy individuals, who make use of tax havens to avoid or evade taxes owed. The 2012 Global Financial Integrity report on *Illicit financial flows from developing countries* shows that developing countries lose around $900billion a year to illicit outflows, or about seven times more than they receive in aid.[238, 239] This money mainly ends up in developed countries. For the very poorest countries this is crippling, with Lesotho for example losing almost half its income via secrecy jurisdictions from 1990-2008. To put the numbers in perspective, according to UNESCO just $24bn of the $900bn lost would be enough to put every child in a developing country through primary and lower-secondary education.[240]

Another way in which the system is designed to favour those who are already wealthy is through the dominance of corporate and wealthy interests in our political system. Since the 1970s, corporations and private interests have increasingly sought to influence and capture the political sphere for their own gain. In the book *Suiting Themselves: How corporations drive the global agenda*, Dr Sharon Beder charts the growth and organisation of these corporate groupings since the Second World War, and how they have not only influenced political decision making, but infiltrated all areas of the political machine.[241] They do this through direct donations to politicians or political causes, by forming quasi-political collectives, and by funding research groups and think tanks.[242, 243, 244] Whilst having the benefit of adding a sense of legitimacy to individual policies, these latter efforts also work to legitimise the whole process of corporate involvement in politics, by allowing politicians to heed big business without appearing to be cronies. This perceived legitimacy accommodates a continuous merry-go-round of personnel between the upper levels of politics and big business, despite the obvious risk of conflicts of interest.[245, 246, 247, 248] Politicians regularly sit on the boards of big companies,[249] while company executives hold government positions,[250, 251] lead government reviews and consultations,[252] hold influential positions in the civil service,[253, 254] as well as in key public-interest bodies,[255] and are afforded special access to ministers,[256] or even the prime minister himself;[257] privileges not afforded to less wealthy people. In some cases, even the thin veil of separation is dispensed with, and lobbyists or company executives directly assume senior roles within government or governing parties.[258, 259] George Monbiot explains it further:

'The political role of corporations is generally interpreted as that of lobbyists, seeking to influence government policy. In reality they belong on the inside. They are part of the nexus of power that creates policy. They face no significant resistance, from either government or opposition, as their interests have now been woven into the fabric of all three main parties'.[260]

As an example, one investigation into the Health and Social Care Bill (legislation introduced to increase the role of the private sector in the NHS) found that over two-hundred parliamentarians had past or present financial links to companies involved in healthcare, but were still allowed to vote on the Bill, which was subsequently made law.[261] Another investigation discovered a scheme between large corporate healthcare providers, a healthcare lobby group, a major national newspaper, a neoliberal think tank, a Conservative MP, and Conservative party donors to (to use their own word) 'orchestrate' a campaign to pressurise the government to push through the Health and Social Care Bill.[262]

We can see that the influence of wealth severely undermines the basis of democracy by allowing the wealthy to have a louder voice than the poor. In this age of 'equality', different genders, ages, and ethnicities are represented in the government, but still no poor people.[263] Researchers at the London School of Economics tracked donations to the Conservative Party between 2001 and 2010 and found that over half of all donation income, or £72million, came from just fifty wealthy donor groups, made up of members of the same family or linked companies.[264] With that level of influence being concentrated in the hands of such a small number of people, it is not a surprise that the interests of the poor are ignored.

This situation has arisen, at least in part, because the corporate and wealthy lobby groups have consistently made the case that wealth is good, that the economy is driven by big business, that big business generates wealth and employs millions of people, and so therefore what is good for big business must be good for the country. There is no doubt some truth in all of this; successful, sustainable, and socially responsible big businesses are a part of a well-functioning economy. The problem is, however, that most big businesses do not have the best interests of the citizens of any country at heart - not even their own employees. They consistently use their influence to argue against government regulation of all kinds, to campaign fiercely against corporation taxes, and to seek to avoid paying the taxes they do owe.[265, 266, 267, 268] They threaten to leave the country should they not get their own way.[269] They argue for a reduction in the size and role of government and the elimination of employment unions, ensuring that government and employees are less well equipped to oppose them in future.[270, 271, 272] They even seek to subvert national democracy through the manipulation and dominance of international trade bodies and rules.[273, 274]

In fact, driven by managerial bonus culture and the need to produce profit to pay out to shareholders (called 'dividends'), wealthy business leaders sometimes don't even have the best interest of their own companies at heart; how else to explain vast managerial rewards that 'verge on larceny'?[275] In *23 things they don't tell you about capitalism*, Ha-Joon Chang explains how the 'unholy alliance' of corporate managers and shareholders cause profits to be increasingly diverted to dividends and share buy-backs, vastly increasing the wealth of both parties, but at the expense of reinvestment in staff, capital expenditure, long-term development, and ultimately company sustainability.[276]

The political activity by the large corporate sector is for one purpose: the dominance of our national and global political and economic systems by the wealthy, at the expense of everyone else in society. Its undertaking ensures the continuing capture of ever more of the Earth's resources for those who already have control over obscene amounts, widening inequality and spreading unhappiness in the process. It is achieved through means of threats, bribes and cronyism that in a fair-minded society may well equate to criminal corruption.[277, 278, 279, 280, 281] Yet the truly worrying thing is that although much of this is done in secret, much is done out in the open without fear of reproach. As JK Galbraith put it, 'What occurs every day is not news'.[282] We have either become desensitised to the extent of control or we feel powerless to act.

Meanwhile, the government pursues austerity measures that continue to undermine the livelihoods of the neediest in society: the poor and unemployed the sick, victims of injustice, and the disabled.[283] At the same time it reduces taxes on those earning over £150,000 a year, and introduces policies that give away £9bn a year in tax cuts to big businesses that already have huge cash reserves.[284, 285] It hopes that tax cuts for the wealthy will 'encourage them to invest' and that the wealth will somehow 'trickle-down' to the rest of society, despite substantial evidence that this does not occur.[286, 287] The government view seems to be that the poor are too rich to work, and the rich too poor. This is clearly not a question of who deserves what. Money translates as a fair approximation of power, and the people of Britain do not work and live on a level playing field. Wages are now so low in relation to the cost of living that the majority of those under the poverty line are from working households.[288] While there will always be a small minority of poor people who deliberately avoid earning an income through work, there are also plenty of wealthy people who have applied themselves no better, benefitting from either the fortune of birth or the hard work of others.

Furthermore, we live in a world of finite resources. In nomadic times, with few people on the planet, and when we were still 'cowboys', our ability to acquire resources was only restrained by the effort we exerted. All resources were effectively 'free' to acquire, provided we were willing to work to obtain them. Once the human population increased however, and with the development of agriculture, humans established territories and came into contact and competition with each other more frequently. Systems were then required to divide the land and the resources contained within it. We have reached the point where, in today's world, there are no longer any 'free' resources; almost all have been charted and distributed and now belong to someone within the system. The few resources that have yet to be discovered, such as those underneath the deep ocean or the ice caps, require such huge resources to chart and extract that only the wealthiest can obtain them.

As a result, we may gain some resources that are passed down to us by our parents or others who are already in the economic system, but the majority of us must earn our livelihoods by offering our labour to someone within the system, in exchange for wealth. Our success and survival depends on the good fortune of nationality, intelligence, appearance, social status, natural ability, and education; or how well equipped we may find ourselves at the end of childhood to fulfil the demands placed on labour by those who own the resources – the wealthiest in society. In our economic system, many are wealthy because they are born into considerable privilege, afforded very high levels of education, have acquired scores of invaluable contacts and, despite working to turn these advantages into substantial wealth, are simply following a very straight-forward path laid out for them. Were they born into a less-favourable situation, it would be unlikely they would acquire such riches. As the famed investor and world's third-wealthiest man Warren Buffet once said, 'If you stick me down in the middle of Bangladesh or Peru or someplace, you find out how much this talent is going to produce in the wrong kind of soil'.[289]

Our economic system must change if we are to live within the sustainable limits of the Earth. Living within these limits means that we can no longer accommodate the mind-boggling levels of inequality that exist within our country and our world. Our system is so unequal because it has been designed, created and controlled, both politically and economically, for the benefit of those who are already vastly wealthy. They use their power and influence to attempt to either separate themselves out at the 'top' of society, or cut loose the worst-off from the bottom, or both, undermining the democratic processes of society in the process. Yet we do not live alone in either a neatly segregated 'public' or 'private' sphere. We are social astronauts on a social spaceship, sharing a finite space with finite resources, and we must make decisions for the good of the whole. In a world of such vast and unhealthy gaps between the richest and the poorest, it makes sense to change our systems and opt for a large redistribution of wealth both within countries and, through tax justice and fairer international trade, between them. This is the only way we can hope to reduce our overall levels of consumption enough to be able to live together sustainably on the Earth, and for our children and grandchildren to have any chance of doing the same.

MAKING CHANGES

THE CHALLENGE for us now is how we go about restructuring our broken system. Economics is an imprecise science; this is evident from the failure of most economists to predict such significant events as stock market crashes or commodity or housing bubbles. This is partly down to incorrect models and assumptions, a fact that is now pointed out on a regular basis in mainstream economic commentaries such as the *Financial Times*.[290] However, it may also be to do with the sheer complexity of the area of study: namely the entire economic activity of every human being within a certain geographical area, and the economic effects of the interactions between them, and also between them and others outside that geographical area – a blatantly impossible task. Macro-economists try to solve this problem by building models and making assumptions, and looking at the inputs and outputs of the system as a whole. This can give indications and identify trends, but it cannot accommodate the 'butterfly effect': the way that small or apparently insignificant actions can create or shape much larger occurrences further into the future. Neither are economists able to accommodate the effects of new types of events, technologies, or interactions that do not already have a place within their models, and so can pass by without being recognised, analysed and accounted for. Whilst the odd renegade economist might be able to predict a major unusual event, learned groups of economists rarely do; possibly due to the fact that the committee consensus, or the 'middle-ground', is by definition unlikely to agree on the likelihood of occurrences towards the extremes of the model.

It is therefore impossible for even the wisest economic sage to predict the economic situation more than a few years in the future with any kind of accuracy. Despite this, there are things that can be known, if not with precision then at least by their general direction of travel. We can, for example, understand that financial crashes tend to occur more frequently in countries with uncontrolled, or even 'out of control' financial services. In other cases we can look to the examples of history, or of other parts of the world, for what might happen in certain situations. So we know from history that people can exist very happily in advanced societies on much lower levels of GDP, such as in the USA during the 1960s. In addition, whilst the neoliberal models have not done a very good job of predicting the current economic state of Britain, when viewed from other perspectives, such as Keynesianism, our economy is behaving much more as expected.

Yet unfortunately we do not have any examples of a modern, developed economy with a capitalist economic system that has attempted to significantly reduce its level of consumption, as proposed here. While there is a growing body of research into what is known as 'stable-state' economics, which is the attempt to limit or freeze growth completely, few apply this idea to the goal of significantly reducing consumption to the levels of forty years ago. How far this reduction could be pushed is unknown and, as a result, whilst I believe that the proposals here could work in reducing consumption while improving wellbeing, it would be incorrect to claim that what follows is the only or complete answer. Economies work in mysterious ways, and any solution will have to be a living, breathing, flexible one that is able to accommodate and adjust for any surprises that may occur. However, amongst this uncertainty it is important to remember that it is not as if the system we currently have is satisfactory, or that civilisation can be sustained without changing it. Neither did the majority hope or choose for our economic system to be how it is. In the words of Paul Hawken: 'No one said, "Wouldn't it be cool to have a juggernaut economy that destroys the capacity of every living system on Earth?"'[291]

All that being said I see no reason to not believe that the following represents, at the very least, a solid contribution to the discussion on how to live within sustainable limits. We must reduce our consumption, and so we must be able to paint a picture of how an economy that thrives while attempting to do that might function. This is not about anti-development, or about going back to a less technological time. History shows that we cannot halt technological progress, and nor would we wish to; the continuing development of technology will be an important tool in helping to limit our environmental impact. Yet we have to recognise that there are limits to what technology can achieve on its own, and if we are to meet the ecological challenges we will also have to develop our relationships with each other, the things we own, and the Earth itself. We will look at these in more detail in later chapters.

There is also an element of these proposals that is about how we might 'pay' for the changes and, as economics in money terms is currently the primary measure of social and political success, it is how this discussion will start. However, we have also seen that money as the medium of analysis must change in time, and hopefully over time accounting methods such as 'green accounting' or others based on communal wellbeing or Earth health will come to replace those we currently use which are, in most part, based on the extraction and destruction of natural resources.

The current state of our economy

The British economy has recently endured over half a decade of stagnation, with no widespread recovery in sight. Tough government austerity measures intended to boost confidence in the economy have done no such thing, and instead stifled growth. This is because in an economic downturn the government plays a key role in stimulating investment. In the absence of investment from households, businesses, and other countries buying UK exports, it falls on the government to take up the slack by investing in the economy. The current government refuses to do this because of ideological reasons and what it perceives to be the high level of sovereign debt, which is also the justification for its policy of public sector cuts.[292] However, we have already found that from a historical perspective UK sovereign debt is not particularly high, either as a percentage of GDP, or by the terms of the outstanding debt: the length of time we have to 'pay it off' and the current costs of the repayments.[293]

Also contrary to the narrative, we have not arrived at the current level of indebtedness by government or public sector overspending. The increase in debt was the result of the economic shock caused by the financial crisis, and the massive costs to the government of bailing out and then propping up the failing banking system. Government policies remain relatively unchanged, both in the face of evidence that they may be restricting growth rather than promoting it, and with the knowledge that the severity of the cuts are placing significant strain on the poorest in society. As a result, tax revenues are struggling to recover, and this is hampering the government's main aim of reducing the deficit: the difference between what it spends, and what it earns in income through taxes and other means during a given year. As of 2014, what the government spends in a year is still over £100bn more than it receives in income.

Running a deficit in any given year is not problematic, and being able to borrow is important for a government, in order to be able to invest in key areas of an economy. It is also important so that private investors who loan to the government, such as pension funds, have somewhere safe to keep some of their money over the long term and earn moderate levels of interest. Like any other debt, a deficit that is too large or too expensive to maintain will be reflected in the unwillingness of investors to lend any further. Yet in the UK, lenders to the government do not seem particularly worried, as underlined by the fact that the government can currently continue to borrow from them at low rates of interest. Despite these conditions, continuing with such a large deficit is not an ideal long-term situation. Whilst even a modest economic recovery would significantly reduce the deficit, its current size indicates that there are some fundamental issues with the allocation of resources in the UK economy.

As of 2014 there are roughly 2.2 million unemployed people in the UK, of which nearly a million are young people.[294] 20% of 16–24 year olds cannot find a job – the third highest level of all developed countries, behind only Greece and Spain.[295, 296] With inflation (the increasing cost of goods and services) taken into account, workers in the UK saw their pay drop by 8.5% between 2009 and 2013, whilst the wealthiest continue to increase their slice of the economic cake.[297, 298] The decline in wages, accompanied by rising inequality, has meant that the median annual wage for a UK worker is now £7,000 lower than it would have been had the wage growth and conditions in the period leading up to the financial crisis continued through to 2013.[299] Living standards will still be 3.5% lower in 2019 than they were in 2009.[300] Depressed wages and booming house prices have led to a household debt crisis, as families dig into their savings or rely on borrowing to make up the shortfall.[301, 302]

The decline in wages also means that, as of 2013, there are *five-hundred thousand* citizens reliant on food banks to meet their basic nutritional needs.[303] Acknowledging this reality, the British Red Cross has begun to distribute food to the poor and hungry in Britain for the first time in 70 years, whilst doctors from the Medical Research Council believe that the accompanied rise in malnutrition points to an impending public health emergency.[304, 305] These outcomes are the direct result of the choice to focus the cuts disproportionately on the poorest and neediest in society.[306] When poverty and hardship of this magnitude occurs in one of the wealthiest countries in the world, the problem is not that there isn't enough money; it's that the money is in the wrong place.

Economic inequality is also reflected geographically, with the poorest areas the ones most affected by austerity measures.[307] Research funded by the Pulitzer Centre on Crisis Reporting found that one of the main effects of austerity was to 'widen the gaps in prosperity between the best and worst local economies across Britain'. It also found evidence that 'the Coalition government is presiding over national welfare reforms that will impact principally on individuals and communities outside its own political heartlands'.[308]

Businesses that could invest in the economy and boost employment are instead sitting on their money, unwilling to invest it because prospects for a return are so poor in the currently stagnant economic climate.[309] The government too are refusing to invest in the economy to get it moving again, and instead of pressuring those with money to put it back into the economy, they are reducing taxes on both the wealthy and big business. Austerity and connected policies are causing structural damage to HMRC, the NHS and education, and legal aid, mental health, debt advice, welfare, and countless other supporting services provided for or commissioned by local councils are being dangerously reduced. The cuts are not just damaging essential services, but the principles and capacity of sound government itself.

The nature of the cuts also displays a frighteningly short-term outlook. Funding for children's services in the UK was cut by £300million in 2011/12, and 2012 saw the closure of the £600m Education Maintenance Allowance scheme, which had previously made it financially viable for tens of thousands of children from poorer backgrounds to attend further education. The combination of these and cuts to key benefits have led UNICEF to predict that a further *four-hundred thousand* children in the UK could be below the poverty line by 2015/16.[310] Research collated in the same UNICEF report shows that lower child wellbeing is linked to consequences...

'...*from impaired cognitive development to lower levels of school achievement, from reduced skills and expectations to lower productivity and earnings, from higher rates of unemployment to increased dependence on welfare, from the prevalence of antisocial behaviour to involvement in crime, from the greater likelihood of drug and alcohol abuse to higher levels of teenage births, and from increased health care costs to a higher incidence of mental illness'.*[311]

According to research by Donald Hirsch at Loughborough University, the current trends could, by 2020, lead to 3.4million children in relative poverty, at a cost of over £35billion in 2012's terms, or 3% of GDP.[312] To suggest that the mitigation of these risks and, in the process, the future economic and social prosperity of the country is not worth an extra £1bn a year now is bizarre; this is less than a penny in the pound on just the very top rate of income tax, or a 2% cut to the defence budget, in exchange for improving the lives of a significant proportion of the UK's poorest children. It is also a fraction of the amount of annual subsidy provided to our banking and financial services sector that, despite minor changes, remains unreformed.

In many cases the costs of pre-emptive support undercut the costs of dealing with the resulting consequences of inaction. It costs about £6,000 a year to send a child to university, about £3,000 a year to college, and even less than that to provide them with a job, as much of what is paid in wages is returned in tax and other contributions elsewhere in the economy, through what is known as the 'multiplier effect'.[313] Yet it costs upwards of £40,000 a year to send someone to prison, for example, and that doesn't include the costs associated with the damage of crime, lost productivity in the economy, and the costs to the victims of crime and their insurance companies, reflected in higher premiums for everyone else.[314] What's more, the consequences of austerity and the resulting structural economic damage can still be felt many decades after they first occur. The economist and *Financial Times* journalist Martin Wolf explains this in an article for the *London Review of Books*:

> *'Austerity has failed. It turned a nascent recovery into stagnation. That imposes huge and unnecessary costs, not just in the short run, but also in the long term: the costs of investments unmade, of businesses not started, of skills atrophied, and of hopes destroyed.'* [315]

This hints at the fundamental flaw of the austerity narrative: that we need to somehow 'save' now so that we can spend later. However, the productivity lost now by not spending can never be spent later. Two million people not working for a year cannot be carried forward to some undetermined point in the future: it is two million people-years of work that is lost forever. Likewise the effect this has on them, their families, and their wider communities cannot be undone. We cannot travel back in time, and so we cannot send money back from the future to employ people that weren't at work when they could have been. The only thing we can do at any point in time is to make sure that as many people as possible are enjoying the benefits of a fulfilling livelihood and prosperous and healthy lives, to the greatest benefit of the wellbeing of the whole country. If we want to see this happen, then we need to make significant changes to the distribution and allocation of resources in our economy.

Changing our financial system

A number of the earlier chapters in this book were dedicated to unpicking our current financial and monetary system. Through the examination of the 'debt imperative' for growth we saw that there is little scope for running a stable, sustainable economy using our current financial system. By contrast, there are numerous advantages to separating out the creation of money from the creation of debt, and moving money from a position of private benefit to one that benefits the public. We can expect a more stable financial system, which should either completely remove, or at least vastly reduce the likelihood of financial crises and cycles of booms and busts.

Then there are the immediate financial benefits. The previous financial crisis cost the government, and by extension our whole nation, a minimum of £1.8tn – or over £3,000 for every man, woman, and child in the United Kingdom.[316] Under a transformed monetary system, a cost of this size would never be incurred again, and neither would the UK economy have to bear the £30-50bn a year in subsidies to the financial sector that it currently provides. In addition, moving the creation of money from private to public control would return the profit from money creation, or seigniorage, back to the government, in order to reduce taxes or provide better public services; amounting to tens of billions of pounds a year.

Lastly, there are other ways of reallocating resources from the financial service sector. 'One-off' levies on bonuses have been used before, generating billions of pounds in revenue, and could easily be used again. Alternatively, taxation on financial products through a universally applied Financial Transaction Tax (FTT), otherwise known as the 'Tobin' or 'Robin Hood' tax, could further aid redistribution. A 0.01% tax on all financial transactions could raise over £8bn a year in the UK. Alternatively, we could opt to tax the riskiest or most 'unsafe' financial transactions such as short-selling, or simply treat all financial products as we do pharmaceutical ones, and test them for their benefits and risks before permitting their use in a more stringently-regulated financial environment. It's impossible to calculate precisely, but it appears quite likely that moving to a new financial system alone could go a long way towards narrowing the current £108bn budget deficit.

Dealing with the tax gap

Expert estimates put the 'tax gap' at over £100bn a year. The tax gap is the difference between what tax could be collected if all taxpayers obeyed the intention of the law, and what is actually collected. It is therefore a measure of all the tax that is avoided, evaded or yet to be paid. Tax evasion means illegally evading the paying of tax, whilst tax avoidance is the exploitation of loopholes or 'grey areas' to avoid paying taxes. Tax avoidance, although technically legal, is contrary to the intention or spirit of the law. Much evasion and avoidance occurs through the use of complicated, confusing, or secret tax arrangements, often by routing money via tax havens.[317]

Britain's position at the centre of a web of global tax havens puts it in a unique position to lead the fight against this unjust system.[318] Changes to the way financial information is exchanged internationally, as well as the clarity with which companies report their finances, are already gathering pace in the European Union and across the international community, led by international groups such as the Tax Justice Network. If enacted fully, these proposals will allow countries to reduce the amount of tax lost by various forms of tax avoidance undertaken by global corporations, and raise billions of pounds in extra revenue. There is also much more that can be done 'closer to home', by changing tax legislation and increasing funding to the public tax-collection body, HMRC. Cuts to HMRC have seen tens of thousands of employees removed from its workforce over the last few years, despite the fact that each HMRC employee pays for their wages many times over in tax collected.[319] In addition, the introduction of a simple anti-avoidance principle into UK legislation, such as that proposed by the MP Michael Meacher, would vastly reduce the amount of tax lost to avoidance.[320] A general anti-avoidance principle removes the 'grey areas' favoured by tax avoiders by declaring that the spirit of tax law must be obeyed, rather than just its technical definition.

It is unlikely that the tax gap could ever be completely eliminated, but through proposals such as the ones outlined above, it is possible that many tens of billions could be recovered. This would vastly reduce the deficit, as well as the burden placed on those in society who pay their taxes in full and on time. Reducing the tax gap will ensure that everyone in society contributes to the country's wellbeing, not just those good citizens that do not seek to avoid paying their taxes.

Moving to a land-based taxation

Another significant change that needs to happen regards the nature of taxation: namely what is taxed and why. The UK currently taxes a whole range of different activities and products at different rates. One of the main taxes is on income, but the UK also taxes general consumption with VAT, property with council tax and stamp duty, vehicles, fuel, alcohol, tobacco, and business profits, to name just a few. There is no stated, overarching aim of taxation other than to, as a simplified explanation, raise revenue for the government to spend.

Some taxes are 'flat-rate', which means that everyone pays the same regardless of wealth. VAT is an example of this, as the standard rate is 20% on qualifying products, regardless of who is buying. Flat-rate taxes such as VAT are regressive, which means they result in those that are less wealthy paying a greater percentage of their income in tax than those who are richer. Because of this flat taxes are far more affordable for the wealthier people in society. Alternatively some taxes are 'progressive', which means that those who have more pay more. This is the intention of income tax, which has a number of increasing rating bands which apply as income increases. There are also taxes that, whilst appearing to be progressive in theory, are not progressive in practice, as those rich enough to afford clever accountants and lawyers can exploit loopholes to avoid some, or all, of what is owed.

Whilst attempts are made to make the tax system progressive rather than regressive, the tax system as a whole doesn't appear to support the values that the country would wish to promote. We do tax some 'bad' things, like alcohol or cigarettes, but we also tax income highly which, regardless of how the tax is stratified, can act as a disincentive to work for some people. We also tax different things at different rates, which can allow accountants and advisers to shift the income of their clients into other forms of wealth that are not taxed as heavily. The complexity of the UK tax system makes it difficult to create a cohesive, progressive taxation policy that would help bring inequality down to levels that enable us to live sustainably. However, perhaps the main reason why the tax system cannot reduce inequality or be truly progressive is that, by focusing on earned income, it fails to effectively tax the main source of wealth: land.

Land is power in more ways than one. In a biological sense, it enables the origination of all energy on Earth: the effect of sunlight acting on the ground, and on plants through the process of photosynthesis. In a socio-political sense, land enables virtually all wealth-producing activities and resources: freshwater, agriculture, mineral extraction, manufacturing, housing, transport, recreation, and countless others. Whoever owns the land owns the wealth and the ability to create it, either directly or through rent-collecting activities. Yet the distribution of land in Britain is hugely unequal, with 69% of all land area owned by just 0.6% of the population.[321] The effect of land on wealth is reflected in the levels of inequality in the UK. When looking at income, the level of inequality is wide enough, with the top 10% earning twenty-four times more than the bottom 10%.[322] However, when considering total owned wealth instead of income, the richest 10% are 850 times wealthier than the poorest 10%.[323]

That inequalities in land distribution should be mirrored in wealth is not hard to understand. Much like the creation of money, land has no cost of production. Its value originates entirely from its scarcity and the competing needs of society for it; yet it is private interests that benefit.[324] The value of land is partly determined by its geographical location in relation to things like rivers or good soil, but this value is enhanced by the behaviours of the rest of the community: through the creation of transport links, population density, shops and amenities, instances of crime, stewardship of the environment, and much more. Land has value almost entirely because of the services provided to it by the wider community. It makes sense, therefore, that the wider community should benefit from it. A tax on the value of land would enable this to happen, and at the same time be the single most direct way of reducing inequality by the redistribution of wealth. It might seem radical, but it is hardly a new idea, as George Monbiot explains:

'In 1909 a dangerous subversive explained the issue thus: "Roads are made, streets are made, services are improved, electric light turns night into day, water is brought from reservoirs a hundred miles off in the mountains – and all the while the landlord sits still. Every one of those improvements is affected by the labour and cost of other people and the taxpayers. To not one of those improvements does the land monopolist, as a land monopolist, contribute, and yet by every one of them the value of his land is enhanced. He renders no service to the community, he contributes nothing to the general welfare, he contributes nothing to the process from which his own enrichment is derived ... the unearned increment on the land is reaped by the land monopolist in exact proportion, not to the service, but to the disservice done." Who was this firebrand? Winston Churchill'.[325]

A Land Value Tax (LVT) would not tax the value of the buildings or other additions on top of the land, but just the land itself. This enables the element that is the result of effort and enterprise – the building of property – to escape taxation, and for tax to be levied just on the element whose value is naturally or communally derived. This might sound complicated to establish, but is in fact much simpler to work out than the value of land and property combined, as it would not need to take into account property-related factors such as the age and condition of the buildings, potential for expansion, and costs of maintenance. A tax on land would replace our current taxes on property such as council tax and stamp duty, and as it is a tax for the redistribution of owned wealth rather than income, it could even replace inheritance taxes.

In some ways LVT appears too good to be true, yet it is very real, and is used at local or regional levels in other parts of the globe including Denmark and the USA, to great benefit. Council tax is deeply regressive, and inheritance tax is often avoided; LVT by contrast, is both deeply progressive and hard to avoid. Stamp duty reinforces geographical imbalances in the economy by making it hard for people to move house to follow economic opportunities; land tax reduces geographical inequalities. It does this by reducing the costs of holding land in areas that are currently under-developed, enabling greater profit to be made, and so attracting economic activity.

LVT is not primarily a tax on homeowners. There are twenty-five million homes in Britain, yet just 4% of total land is owned by Britain's seventeen million owner-occupiers.[326] The majority of those that own and live in their own home would likely see their overall tax burden reduced, not increased, by a move to Land Value Taxation. LVT would also be of great benefit to society by reducing the costs of housing in general. By raising the cost of holding large amounts of land for speculative purposes, it would ensure that land is redistributed more equally. Fewer people would be able to afford to keep large amounts of land for themselves, meaning that there would be more to go around for everyone else, reducing its cost.

Whilst the idea of 'fair' is subjective in most real life situations, a tax on land seems the fairest basis for a taxation system, as the amount of land is fixed. What's more, the historical ownership of land in Britain is almost impossible to establish, as a result of changes in ownership through conflicts and policies such as the Enclosure Acts. As Monbiot writes, 'Most of the land in this country, if we go back far enough, was seized from other people, often, in the case of the commons, from entire communities.'[327] A study paper from the LabourLeft political group provides more historical context:

'Where land was in much demand, it would be allocated more or less according to need through various systems of customary tenure. The land was yours as long as you used it, but it could be taken over or re-allocated if you did not. Such systems still exist in parts of Africa and other regions. The private ownership of land – especially when highly concentrated among a few wealthy individuals and families, as in Britain – more often than not, can be traced to its outright theft at some stage by those with political and coercive powers.' [328]

Land Value Tax reflects the reality that we live on an island, Great Britain, whose land is the source of public wealth, and which we must share between us if we are all to prosper in the future. Britain is a country of sixty million acres, not far off one acre each, and that one acre has to provide food, energy, housing, transport infrastructure, public goods such as hospitals, schools, and administration, recreational land, and industrial and commercial land such as factories and shops. On top of this, there must be enough land left over to disseminate our wastes, and a certain amount of land isn't really useable for many of those things. So our land, as a major resource, is limited. With only one acre each we cannot all live in a palatial mansion on many-acred grounds. As the columnist Simon Jenkins writes, 'Whilst everyone would like a cottage in the country, there would be no country if everybody had one.' [329]

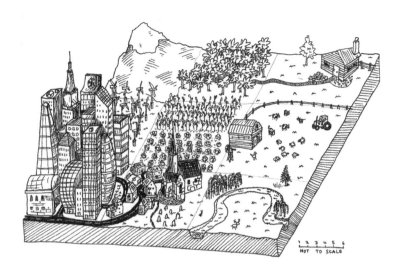

NOT TO SCALE

There are plenty of other benefits to a Land Value Tax. Taxing all land, including plots that are empty or unused, would ensure that all land is returned to effective use, rather than being hoarded for speculative purposes. This would keep prices low and stable, and reduce the likelihood of 'bubbles' occurring. It would lead to more compact towns and avoid urban sprawl, and encourage the redevelopment of unsightly brownfield sites, helping to regenerate post-industrial cities. The extra cost of holding empty land would encourage construction companies to build on at least some of the four hundred thousand plots they already hold and have permission for, but aren't building on because they're waiting for prices to rise. The cost of housing would reduce, making a world of difference to young people and those not yet on the property ladder. It would enable people to own their own home much sooner, reduce the cost of housing in relation to wages, and so raise living standards. If someone couldn't afford to pay LVT, then it could be deferred until the property is sold at a later date, such as may be the case with pensioners who wish to stay in the same homes until the end of their lives, or with others who may be 'asset rich' but 'income poor'.

The greatest benefit of Land Value Tax is its potential to reduce inequality by redistributing wealth.[330] Not only is LVT hard to avoid, but a study in 2002 found that it had the potential to provide about half of government revenue, enough to completely replace income tax, corporation tax, capital gains tax, inheritance tax, stamp duties and council taxes combined.[331] Whilst we don't have to choose to completely eliminate all the above taxes, it is apparent that not only could LVT effectively and efficiently tax the greatest levels of wealth in our country at source, it would also help simplify the tax system.

What the above changes to our economic systems show is that austerity is a choice, not a necessity. Far from being bankrupt, Britain as a whole is a supremely wealthy country; one that would have no trouble whatsoever providing the services needed for high levels of wellbeing for its entire population, and to bring children out of poverty. All that is required is for the government to decide to redistribute more of the resources from those who have captured quite phenomenal levels of wealth to those who have very little. Considering the absurd level of inequality and the increasing poverty for those at the bottom of the ladder, there is a strong moral case for redistribution. Yet as we have seen there is also an environmental case; we must eliminate such vast inequalities if we are to have any hope of living together sustainably on the Earth.

TOMORROW

DESPITE POWERFUL VESTED INTERESTS, there are no fundamental obstacles within our financial and economic systems
that might prevent us shaping our societies and country differently, provided we find the political will to make the necessary
choices. Rather than being a complex and impenetrable maze
that we cannot hope to make sense of, our monetary system
can be understood more than enough for us to make use of it
as a tool for our national purposes, and for the benefit of all
rather than the profits of a few.

This means that not only can it serve our purposes; it can
serve the purposes of our planet. We no longer have to put
environmental needs subserviently below those of the economy; we can instead shape our economy to allow us to flourish
within the limited resources available on our finite planet.
We do not have to dedicate our lives to the blind pursuit of
economic growth at all costs. Not only is continual economic
growth an impossible goal, in chasing it we are severely damaging the capacity of the planet to sustain human life.

As we discovered earlier in this book, few politicians today
are willing to set out their values and their vision for the future
and to talk about the cohesive set of policies they would put
in place to bring that about. Politics is increasingly short term
and, either because of austerity, the challenges of globalisation
or otherwise, governments appear to doubt their own ability to
shape a better world for the good of the people they govern. The

ideas behind this, driven by neoliberal thinking, often describe our existence as a 'race' or even a 'war', as if there's nothing we can do but run as fast as we can. This is disempowering for everyone. The current government talks about austerity and has repeatedly said there is 'no plan B', despite the disastrous impacts the policy is having on the UK economy and society.[332] The synopsis for one recent policy booklet from British MPs, *Britannia Unchained*, goes as far as saying:

'Britain is at a crossroads which will define our place in the world for generations. From our economy, to our education system, to social mobility and social justice, we must learn the rules of the 21st century, or we face an inevitable slide into mediocrity'.[333]

The implication here is that the rules have already been set, and we have no choice but to obey them. How depressing! The accountant and economist Richard Murphy calls this 'the cowardly State', as its elected politicians believe there is little that government can do to make things better; their only solution is to leave things to the market. As he writes in his book *The Courageous State*:

'...we did not end up in this situation by chance: this development of the cowardly state represents a seemingly coordinated and certainly consistent pattern of policy that has, despite the changes of political parties in power, continued unabated for an extraordinary period of time'.

As a result he believes that:

'...there has been an enormous loss of confidence in politicians in the UK. That's an entirely rational reaction by the UK electorate. If the politicians standing for office seem to have no confidence in the processes of government that they wish to run, they're hardly going to present a confident front, or even a competent front, to the electorate. After all, any rational person

might wonder why someone is desperate for a job in an organisation they appear to despise and are setting out to destroy'.[334]

Instead of a lack of conviction and vision from our politicians, there is a desperate need for people with conviction and, as importantly, imagination to help envision the kind of country we want to live in. Indeed, we do not need to place limits on our imaginations. As stated before, the country works the way it does because of decisions made by people, and if people have made decisions, then people can change them, or make different ones.

We are therefore at the point where we need to cast our minds forward rather than back. What are we living for? What kind of world do we want to live in? What do we want tomorrow to look like? It is only when we answer these questions that we can plan that world into being, and take the steps necessary to get there.

THE MACHINE

IN PREVIOUS CHAPTERS we identified that we cannot continue to grow our economy by producing and consuming more stuff, if we are to live within the environmental limits of the Earth that sustains us. However, we've found that embedded within our economic system are two 'imperatives for growth' – an efficiency imperative and a debt imperative – that make restraining or reversing growth incredibly difficult, if not impossible. As we've examined the workings of our financial system we've seen that it can be changed, and that this would remove the requirement for growth that our debt-as-money system creates. The efficiency imperative however provides a further challenge.

We considered how the only 'solution' to the problems created by increasing efficiency has been the prescription of yet more unsustainable growth. How the only apparent option is to keep employing the same number of people, but produce more and more stuff: the growth imperative. But there is another option that we have not yet discussed in detail: working less and sharing that work around.

In earlier stages of development of human society, increased efficiency was much needed. People were less protected against nature, against hardship, and against diseases; they were still cowboys battling to survive. The levels of development and consumption by the collective endeavours of humanity in societies across the globe were still well within the natural limits of the Earth to sustain them. There was always the possibility that more labour would increase the wealth of the whole, if only it was available. Over time efficiency, achieved through the discovery and development of more productive processes and technologies, enabled otherwise poor societies to develop themselves, lift themselves out of subsistence and reduce individual workloads. It introduced the notion of leisure time and freed people to have a choice about the activities or work they pursued. Increases in efficiency, and increases in the amount of labour added to the collective wealth. Then, around the middle of the last century, the situation changed, and human development tipped the balance.

Improvements in medicine and healthcare had allowed humans to live longer. Advances in productive efficiency brought about by the industrial and scientific revolutions had led to huge increases in total production, and therefore consumption and wealth, especially in the developed world. However, by the 1970's collective human society had reached the point where it was digging up, consuming, and throwing away more than the Earth could sustain; we had surpassed our sustainable share of 'global hectares'. Ever since that point, additional production has become increasingly unsustainable. It damages the capacity of the Earth to support future generations, not just to exist, but to thrive in the way that we have done recently. Everyone alive today is entitled to their share of the resources available from within the limits imposed by the sustainable productive capacity of the Earth, yet we are already producing far more than we can sustain. From known levels of unemployment we can conclude that we have become so efficient that we can produce the maximum amount allowed within sustainable limits without using anywhere near humanity's total supply of labour.

This doesn't mean that we can't ever become any more efficient but rather that, as we cannot afford more growth in production and consumption, greater efficiency is pointless unless the benefit is harnessed in the form of less overall labour. Yet as we have discussed, less labour in our current economy tends to mean that some people are laid off of work, which causes increasing unemployment and the societal problems and costs that accompany it. A potential solution therefore is to reduce the amount of labour by ensuring that *everyone* works less, so that the total availability of work is shared around. It seems that any developed, but sustainable economy that wishes to keep unemployment low must either be more inefficient in comparison with current possible levels of production, or reduce working hours across the economy, or both.[335]

Unfortunately, working fewer hours would have an impact on wages. We have already established that we cannot all own yachts or be billionaires, and that living within the environmental limits of our planet means consuming less. This means that by our current methods, which measure wealth simply as production and consumption, we have no choice but to be less wealthy in the future. This trend can however be mitigated to a significant degree by adjusting our understanding of wealth to greater prioritise a broader measure of wellbeing that includes not just how much money we have in the bank, but the health and value of our environment, how resilient our communities are to economic or environmental challenges, how much leisure time we have, and the opportunities we have to explore the richness of human existence. We will visit this idea in the remaining chapters. From an economic perspective, however, we can mitigate our reduction in national consumption by sharing out the benefits of efficiency more equally. By shifting more wealth from the owners and those that have the most, to everyone else. By reducing profits that the richest individuals make and increasing wages for the majority. This is not just out of the need to reduce the impact that the reduction in wealth and consumption will have. If increasingly efficient societies are going to prosper it is essential that the demand for goods and services is more evenly spread across society.[336]

This is because, as previously mentioned, workers are not simply producers, but also customers and consumers. Producing at the lowest possible cost by squeezing wages will result in the most profit in the short term for a single company, yet in the long term, and for the wider economy, it leads to stagnant demand and widespread societal issues. It supresses demand across the economy for the very goods that companies are trying to sell in order to earn their profit. An individual company may succeed by pursuing this strategy in the short term, but by the time wages have been squeezed across the whole economy, demand for products will fall, reducing profits anyway. We are living through a period which evidences the result of stagnant wages. The ratio of wages to profits has plummeted in the last twenty years. Inequality has increased, whilst business investment has decreased.[337] The economy is in need of significant investment, whilst companies sit on £700bn of profits, unable to invest in increasing production because there is no one to buy their products when they do.[338] This is the result of the austerity narrative of earlier chapters. It is an ideal opportunity for the government to step in and legislate for the improvement of wages, the taxation of un-utilised wealth that includes corporate profits, and the reduction of poverty. Companies might complain in the short term, but in the long term it suits everyone. It makes little sense for a single company to invest alone, but it makes sense if every company does it together.

The choices are more apparent when considering an efficiency-related thought exercise. As our technology has developed we have devised more efficient processes, and more and more of the work that used to be done by humans is now done by machines. This includes not just manual production, such as on car production lines or in construction, but also in retail with online shopping, and in service industries with the internet and automated call centres. This trend has two effects:

firstly, it reduces the number of humans needed in any given productive task; secondly, it concentrates the financial profit available from that production in the hands of fewer and fewer people. If the owner of a car company has more robots and fewer people to employ, then the benefit of that profit is shared with fewer people. After all, whilst they need some maintenance, robots don't have buses to catch or a family to feed.

Now let's imagine that this trend continues: that efficiency, driven by technological developments, continues to improve. Centuries from now, efficiency and technology have driven a world where more and more of production is automated, where cheaper machines continue to replace more expensive labour, and where, in the name of efficiency, separate processes of production are joined together into ever bigger automated systems, taking advantage of the efficiencies of scale. Eventually, the vast majority of the jobs in the world are done by a single gigantic, interconnected machine. There is no space for human inefficiency or mistakes. We have reached 'maximum efficiency'. Now, let's imagine what this world will look like if the benefits from the improvement in efficiency accrue only to the owner of the machine, or alternatively, if the benefits are shared around.

In our imagined scenario, if increased efficiency is allowed to lead to ever increasing unemployment, with profits always accruing to a small number of 'owners', then we end up with a system where one person, or the few people who own the machine take all the benefits from all the resources on the planet, stockpile stupendous levels of wealth, and everyone else gets nothing. Humans will have created a world that puts efficiency and machines above everything, including humanity itself. Humans will suffer and die, and we will have developed our technology at the expense of our lives and our livelihoods. There is no point and no value to humanity in this scenario, and there is little value in the machine either, because there would be no-one who could afford to buy or make use of what it produced. All of the ingenuity of human life will have been reduced to a single, ultimate, non-human mechanism.

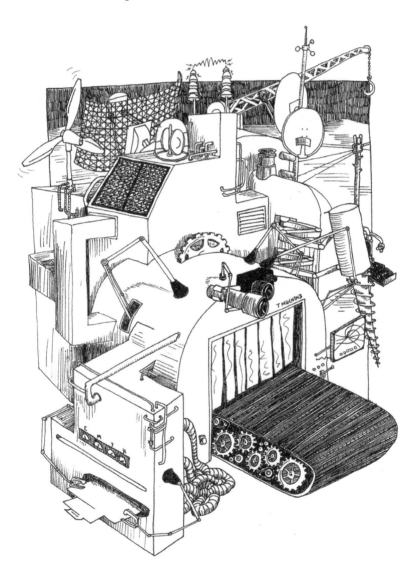

The alternative scenario, however, is one where labour is shared out relatively evenly, wages are maximised instead of profits, and the ownership of our production is more evenly distributed. As efficiency develops, people will work less and less, but still retain the benefits of that automated process that has replaced labour. By the time the single 'machine' stage had been reached, no one would work very much, if at all, but everyone would still be able to prosper and flourish, and enjoy the collective benefits of the technological advances in efficiency. We would spend little time working, and we would have the free time to shape our lives around the communities and activities that we wished, to bring us the most happiness.

Now it's quite possible that neither of these scenarios seem particularly wonderful, so perhaps it is fortunate that real life is more complex and nuanced than this. Whilst we don't want to be cast aside and see our very existence sacrificed to a robot, neither would most of us choose to live a life where our needs would be satisfied without requiring us to work or develop further ingenuity. The failure of communism as an economic system reminds us of the dangers of losing the freedom to create, innovate, and self-determine. As appealing as it might sound to start with, not being productive in one way or another can rob us of our sense of worth and meaning. We can get bored and apathetic just 'sitting around'. The philosopher Michael Foley explains this point in *The Age of Absurdity: why modern life makes it hard to be happy*: 'As Buddha, Spinoza, Rilke, and Frederick Herzberg have observed, we are born not to be lilies of the field but to seek out the difficult and to strive for it constantly'.[339]

We've explored how increasing efficiency not only drives unsustainable growth, but can lead to increasing unemployment which, aside from the societal issues this leads to, can rob people of meaningful work – a crucial part of human existence. Recognising the flaw in the rush towards ever-increasing efficiency should enable us to question the way it is so forcefully pursued from all points of the political spectrum. Couched in these austere times as 'saving money', efficiency is demanded of every government department, local council, university, and many more organisations besides, and appears to be valued above anything else. In the name of efficiency, people are made unemployed, wages are frozen, human jobs are replaced by machine operations, the quality of services is reduced, and the quality of life undermined. Our politicians appear to ignore these systemic causes, and instead blame unemployment on the laziness of the unemployed. However, the logic follows that if we wish to become more efficient whilst also living sustainably within the limits of our planet, we have no choice but to reduce working hours, and share around the benefits of what employment we do have.

We can now see that we do not need any more efficiency in order to satisfy our needs, in fact quite the opposite; increased efficiency is, under our current system of allocating work and its benefits, reducing the possibility that all humans can prosper and enjoy meaningful labour. Efficiency has given to us with one hand but is now picking our pockets with the other. The 'machine' allegory shows us the folly of not deliberately intervening to share out the benefits of ownership more widely than is typical within a capitalist economic system. It also shows us the possibility of sharing the benefits of efficiency in the form of less, but more meaningful and more evenly-distributed work.

It's fortunate then that working less can, rather than being a negative development, lead to countless benefits for society and individuals. Many of us intuitively feel like we are stuck in the 'rat race', with the accompanying stress and tiredness, and the sense that life is passing us by. The New Economics Foundation research group has examined these issues, and believes that the benefits of getting out of the rat race are so great that despite the inevitable drop in consumption, the whole country would be better off if everyone dropped to a twenty-one hour working week.[340] As the report puts it:

'A 'normal' working week of 21 hours could help to address a range of urgent, interlinked problems: overwork, unemployment, over-consumption, high carbon emissions, low well-being, entrenched inequalities, and the lack of time to live sustainably, to care for each other, and simply to enjoy life'.[341]

This is clearly a far cry from the unquestioning pursuit of efficiency in the name of unsustainable economic growth.

The thought of such a wholesale change in lifestyle might seem dramatic, but perhaps this is only because we have become so used to the idea that we must work as hard and as long as possible in order to make sure that we 'win the global race', without thinking very much about what that might mean. We are not rats though, regardless of how often we may struggle to see beyond the daily treadmill. There may not be an overarching 'meaning of life' to which we can all agree, but few of us would truthfully claim that we are happy to simply work as hard as possible in order to secure the resources to be able to consume as much as we can before we die. Life holds more for us than this.

TECHNOLOGY

WEALTH, as defined by our current measure of GDP, is production and consumption. We dig up minerals or harvest crops from the ground. We might then process them into new products, combine them together, or burn them to produce the energy needed to transform other products. Whatever processes they go through, these resources are ultimately 'consumed'; we eat them, or burn them, or use them and then discard them. In some cases, often with the addition of more resources in the form of energy, these consumed resources can be recycled or re-used. In many cases they cannot.

We explored in earlier chapters that money itself is not wealth: wealth is what money can buy us, and what we therefore consume. Yet we cannot keep increasing what we dig up out of the ground and consume. Instead we must reduce it drastically. Calculations based on a paper in the journal Nature by eight European environmental scientists have found that, if we are to keep within the limits of the capacity of the Earth in respect to atmospheric CO_2, we must leave four-fifths (80%) of all known deposits of hydrocarbons (Oil, Gas, etc) in the ground; never mind the deposits that we are yet to discover.[342] Achieving this requires an unprecedented reduction in current levels of consumption, and so by our current definition, wealth.

We cannot reduce consumption simply by 'advancing' our economy. The UK economy has transformed quite dramatically in the last forty years, from an emphasis on manufacturing-

159

based industry to 'high-level' service-based work; yet our level of consumption is ever higher, rising by 20% between 1990 and 2008.[343] What we consume now is more likely to come from Beijing than Birmingham.[344] This is not really surprising; everything produced in the mixed economy of goods and services is ultimately underpinned by the production of goods. After all, everyone in the economy needs to eat, heat their home and buy clothes, and most will buy a TV, use the internet, or go on holiday, regardless of whether they work for a bank or on a factory production line. We cannot survive by eating financial advice, or fuel our cars with the time we spend on the phone to call centres.

What's more, whilst more efficient technology might help our plight, we cannot expect it to save us on its own. We might hope that technology can help us improve the 'material efficiency' of our goods, which means using less physical material, or less energy in the production process, to produce the same outputs. This is the kind of efficiency we mean when we talk about more fuel-efficient engines in cars, for example: we can make the same amount of fuel power the car for longer. Unlike labour efficiency, material efficiency does not come with a requirement that we keep growing. In fact, as it results in using less of the Earth's resources to produce the same amount of product, it is regularly seen as a good thing. Greater material efficiency is often seen as a central pillar in the 'green' strategies to limit climate change and reduce human impact on the Earth's systems. However, like labour efficiency, it is far more complex an issue in practice than might be first assumed.

For example, there is evidence that increasing fuel efficiency of aircraft engines does not necessarily mean that the air travel industry consumes less. It can simply mean that air travel becomes cheaper, which in the long term actually leads to increased fuel use as people get used to cheaper flights, or believe they are now 'good value', and so take more of them: a trend known as the 'Khazzoom-Brookes Postulate'.[345] This perceived 'good value' could even mean that air travel is used more frequently in the place of other, less polluting forms of travel.[346] Similarly, despite adverts regularly referring to the idea of efficiency, most industries do not take advantage of the material efficiency available.

Although individual goods in some industries, such as computing, may be getting smaller and lighter, most industries generate their profits by driving the short-term 'fashion' aspect of products, rather than their long-term function. The term 'planned obsolescence' describes how products such as mobile phones can be deliberately designed to break after a certain

period of time, so that we are forced to buy new ones. Very few things are 'designed to last' anymore. From a material efficiency point of view, there's little to be gained from a 5% or 10% reduction in the used materials for a single product if that product is deliberately designed to need replacing in its entirety several times more frequently than it needs to be. What's more, even where products *are* produced and used more efficiently, the money saved from purchasing them is often used to purchase additional products that wouldn't have been bought otherwise, wiping out or exceeding the initial efficiency gains – a situation environmental economists call 'rebound'.[347, 348]

It is also apparent that on a macro-economic level (looking at the economy as a whole), there is little evidence that improvements in material and technological efficiency have resulted in an overall reduction in energy use and consumption – a trend known as 'de-coupling'. This is because, much like labour efficiency, technological efficiency provides the producer with two choices: they can either earn the same profit by producing less, or earn more profit by producing more. The second option is almost always taken, not least because, when in competition with a similar producer, the largest company with the most profit to reinvest is more likely to survive. It's quite possible that the advantages accrued from improving efficiency are, via the rebound effect and the drive for profits, responsible for the lack of progress in reducing our resource use overall.

The lack of progress in de-coupling resource use from production is demonstrated in research looking at the connection between wealth and the physical limits of the environment. Despite huge advances in technology and efficiency, research shows that global wealth and global energy use have stayed inextricably tied together over the entirety of the last forty years.[349, 350] This is strong evidence that we cannot expect increases in material efficiency to lead to decreases in resource and energy use on a global scale. This should enable us to take a fresh look at the solutions provided by technology and realise that they are only useful if they are combined with regulation and applied in a way that allows us to limit our production and consumption, rather than allowing our appetite for stuff to increase unrestricted.

It seems apparent then that technology alone will not save us. To thrive in the future the human race must get used to consuming less; we must become 'less wealthy'. Yet this needn't be worrying. It is not just essential, but thankfully very possible, that we can thrive and flourish in the future despite consuming less, and even find ourselves better-off than we are now.

HAPPINESS

IT IS APPARENT that we must re-evaluate the idea of 'wealth', and move away from measuring it in terms of how much of the Earth's resources we produce and consume. The human story tells us that there is no reason why we all have to consume more and more in order to thrive. In fact there is very little correlation between wealth and wellbeing beyond the meeting of our most basic needs and those of our family.[351] Yet despite the substantial body of literature on the sources of wellbeing, our systems are structured in such a way that we live to try and maximise our money, even if this leads to unhappiness.

Studies of economic history show that it is possible for us to flourish whilst consuming far less than we do today. Economist David C. Korten marshals the evidence in *When Corporations Rule the World.* Studies by Daly and Cobb of the US economy between 1960 and 1986 found that individual wellbeing in the USA peaked in 1969, and then plateaued and fell until 1986, despite the average GNP per person growing by 35% during the same period.[352] Korten reports that in the UK, Douthwaite found that for the period of doubling of national wealth between 1954 and 1989:

'...it quickly became apparent that almost every social indicator had worsened over the third of a century the experiment had taken. Chronic disease had increased, crime had gone up eight fold, and unemployment had soared'.

Korten himself adds that:

'We might apply a similar test to the more than fivefold increase in global output since 1950. The advocates of growth persistently maintain that economic growth is the key to ending poverty, stabilizing population, protecting the environment, and achieving social harmony. Yet during this same period, the number of people living in absolute poverty has kept pace with population growth: both have doubled. The ratio of the share of the world's income going to the richest 20% to that going to the bottom 20% has doubled. And indicators of social and environmental disintegration have risen sharply nearly everywhere.' [353]

As we've discussed, having money that can never be spent is pointless. It therefore isn't money that we want, but what money can buy us: what it can bring or add to our lives. That might be physical objects like nice clothes or a car or houses, but it is just as likely to be status or recognition or power. Perhaps we see how the lifestyles of the rich are portrayed and we dream of living like that. The problem with this is that whilst having things can make us happy, there is a 'law of declining utility' regarding stuff, which is the phrase that economists use to describe how the more and more things we have, the less additional pleasure each one of those things brings us. For example, if you live in a cold place and don't have a coat, you will be cold and miserable. As a result, buying and owning a coat will make a huge difference to your quality of life and you'll feel much happier. Owning five more coats though won't bring you five times more pleasure. What's more, even if you do particularly enjoy your fifth coat, the chances are you'll rarely think about the others, and only 'enjoy' them on the very few days of the year that you remember you have them and choose to wear them instead. The money spent on each purchase brings a diminishing amount of additional happiness. In addition, if we are unhappy for non-physical reasons like a broken relationship, then buying things to try and make us happy is unlikely to make more than a fleeting difference.

The poor relationship between owning stuff and happiness is well known in the advertising industry. It is the role of advertising not to simply sell products, but to create desire. This is done through showing people unattainable or impossible dreams, and then suggesting that by purchasing a particular product this dream could be reached. It may at first seem important that the dream should be made attainable so that happiness can be experienced, and so the customer will not feel misled. The problem for advertisers is if the products made the buyer genuinely happy, then they would have no reason to buy any more. It is therefore essential that the dream is impossible, and the desire never satisfied. One of the aims of advertising is cultivating unhappiness because, as environmentalist Alistair McIntosh puts it, 'humans who know what makes for a worthwhile life make bad consumers.'[354] The link

167

between consumption and happiness was snappily summarised by the economist Tim Jackson during a talk at the annual TED conference in 2010, when he said that, through advertising, 'people are being persuaded to spend money we don't have, on things we don't need, to create impressions that won't last, on people we don't care about'.[355]

The quote also hints at another reason why we consume as much as we do. We want to be rich as we believe it will bring us happiness through helping us acquire recognition, influence, or other social benefit. This can be a powerful driver for acquiring wealth, as our social status matters greatly to us. What the research shows though is that we can recognise that it is not the wealth itself that brings us status, but our relative wealth in comparison with other people. In an experiment, people were asked whether they would prefer to live in a world where they earned $50,000 and others earned $25,000 or one where they earned $100,000 and others earned $250,000. A majority of those asked opted for the first scenario where they had less income but were richer in comparison.[356] The problem with attempting to improve happiness through relative status is that by definition, 50% of us are always below average, whether that be when measuring wealth or status or power. Because of this, a society's collective happiness will be greatly affected by how wide the gap in status and power is between people who live in it.

This is the root of the message in the seminal book *The Spirit Level*. Pulling together a vast array of research, Richard Wilkinson and Kate Pickett show that people in less equal societies are more likely to be anxious, less trusting of others, and to be mentally ill than people in more equal societies. This is because people in less equal countries are less able to approach what they see as an aspirational level of living within their own social environment.[357] Less equal countries also have higher rates of obesity, infant mortality, drug use, teenage births, homicides, and imprisonment than more equal ones, as well as lower life expectancy, social mobility, and child educational performance. What is most insightful is that these health and social problems are the result of greater income *inequality*, not income itself. This explains why, in any society, richer people will be happier than poorer people, yet over time richer countries are no happier than poorer ones.[358] It also shows why income and consumption are such a poor measure of success in any country, and why it makes little sense to have growth in consumption as a policy target. If that growth occurs in a way that increases inequality rather than reduces it, then it is likely to lead to greater health and social problems and lower levels of wellbeing.

We can further understand why wealth doesn't make us happy, either when exchanged for more stuff or as a proxy for social status, when looking at what it is that *does* make us happy. A movement called Action for Happiness has assembled research on happiness and wellbeing, and has found that only about 10% of what makes up our overall happiness levels is actually related to the stuff we have or our physical environment.[359] Roughly half of our overall happiness is accounted for by our genetic makeup, but about 40% is accounted for by how we choose to spend our time and the choices that we make. What this means is that we can cultivate happiness, rather than it being something that we cannot influence, or just the psychological consequence of what happens to us.

Happiness can be viewed as a discipline, the attainment of which has been the study of countless philosophers throughout human history.[360] It's not about repeating some kind of 'self-help' mantra, and it is not just about seeing the glass as half-full. It is about learning what it is we can do to be happy, and then deliberately taking action to ensure we gain the benefit. A government-commissioned report summarised the multi-disciplinary work of over four-hundred scientists across the world and found what it named the 'Five ways to wellbeing': connecting with people around us, being active, taking notice of the world, learning continually, and giving or sharing.[361] These five 'ways' are also contained in what the Action for Happiness group has identified as the 'Ten keys to happier living' that we can all do to improve our happiness. The group lists these as: giving, enjoying relationships, exercising, appreciating the world around us, trying new activities, having direction and goals, building resilience, focusing on positives, accepting ourselves and our lives, and searching for meaning.[362] Some of these are self-explanatory, and some may require a little more thought. We might particularly relate to some, and less to others. All of them can tell us something more about ourselves, our humanity, and the world in which we live; but only if we care to explore them more deeply and practice them more frequently. Thankfully many of us already know about these 'keys', either consciously or not, and enjoy the benefits of good relationships or trying out new things for example. However, I doubt very much that anyone has all of these mastered, and I suspect most of us could benefit greatly from considering these more in our daily lives.

By developing the mind-set required for happiness, it becomes a lot less daunting to face a world of less consumption and less stuff. There is clearly the capacity for us to become much happier individually on a much smaller environmental footprint. The consumption habit will still be a hard one to kick though, and if we're to seriously reduce the amount that we consume, we will have to not just choose the things that we do have more wisely, but develop a new relationship with things in general.

Consumption in our society is driven by predatory advertising that impresses on us a cycle of fashion and endless variety. It requires us to constantly acquire new things, whether or not we actually need them.[363] As previously mentioned, however, acquiring new things cannot satisfy us, and from the advertiser's perspective it must never satisfy us, or else we wouldn't buy any more stuff. Our relationship with new things is therefore temporary and, without any lasting investment, the short-term buzz that comes from acquiring them quickly wears off. We 'love' new things, but only until the next new thing comes along, after which the 'old' new thing is discarded to the back of the cupboard and forgotten, or thrown away. A new kind of relationship with stuff however would look very different. Described as the 'New Materialism', it is about a love of things, not for the temporary buzz of instant acquisition, but of the depth of relationship that can come from having things for a long time, from cherishing them, and from investing in them through maintaining, repairing or reusing them over and over.[364] It is about re-learning the skills that more of us possessed before the division of labour on factory assembly lines and the increased use of machines in production.

Reusing and repairing things requires us to learn new skills, to have patience and take time over our tasks. It brings us satisfaction through developing ourselves, it allows us to express our creativity, and helps us stay active. Learning new things can also encourage human interaction and sharing, through the development of teacher-apprentice friendships and learning communities. Developing this kind of relationship with the things that we have appears to check off a large number of the keys for happier living. Rather than being the austere and miserable cousin of consumer culture, this alternative approach to having things is a far healthier, more joyful, and more fulfilling way to live. Making, creating, and mending things brings people together, and the social cooperation and sharing it entails is intrinsically rewarding. By contrast, economist and author Andrew Simms finds that:

'...in study after study, people who are more oriented to extrinsic, materialistic values are less likely to be satisfied with life. They experience fewer "pleasant emotions", more distress, anxiety and *depression, are more prone to narcissism and substance abuse, and are more likely to experience negative emotions like being "angry, scared and sad"*.[365]

Perhaps we should have seen this coming. Over thirty years ago, the ground-breaking psychiatrist M. Scott Peck published *The Road Less Travelled*, in which he identified the rejection and fear of difficulty as the root cause of much mental illness. To combat this, he found that one of the key disciplines essential for a mentally-healthy life is delaying gratification, which means turning down a lesser reward now, or the easier path in the short term, for a greater reward later on. It is the same reasoning behind the 'New Materialism'. Advertising-driven consumer culture is all about the 'now'. It is about immediate satisfaction and gratification, but the feeling never lasts and, especially if that consumption is debt fuelled, can lead to difficulties later on. Some people even turn to consumption in an addictive way in an attempt to directly counter or mask the difficulties experienced in other areas of their lives: something we've come to commonly describe as 'retail therapy'. By contrast, choosing to take the more challenging route of learning skills and developing a new relationship with the stuff that we have will take longer, be more challenging, and require much more of us but, because of this, will be immensely more satisfying and rewarding. As Michael Foley puts it in *The Age of Absurdity*:

> '*But, for the age that expects everything to be easy, the most crucial revelation is that everything worthwhile is difficult. In fact, attempts to find easy solutions will cause the very problems these attempts were meant to evade*'.[366]

So we needn't be afraid of living in a world with less consumption; it is not just essential for a sustainable future, but helpful for a mentally healthy one. We might be less wealthy in terms of GDP, our current measure, but we can be far richer in terms of our overall happiness and wellbeing. The famous economist JK Galbraith put it like this:

> '*The best part of the human past is the artistic, literary, religious and scientific accomplishments that emerged from societies where they were the measure of success. The art of Florence, the wonderful civic creation that is Venice, William Shakespeare, Richard Wagner and Charles Darwin, all came from communities with a very low Gross Domestic Product. It was their good fortune that they were free from the constraints of salesmanship and managed public response. Today it is only in the protected cultural, artistic, educational and scientific aspects of life that we have more compelling tests of human achievement than money*'.[367]

Money is a poor measure of the things that are most important to humans and humanity, and the things that make us happiest. Yet there is a lack of understanding of these alternative ways of living and of achieving happiness and wellbeing in our consumerist society. Embedding some of the ten 'keys' to happier living identified by Action For Happiness into our national policy and media debates would be a good start. Whilst the focus of many of the 'keys' is on individual action, one in particular appears to be especially relevant to wider society, yet is possibly also the least understood. This is the 'search for meaning' – known in philosophy, religion, and much literature as 'transcendence'.

It is unsurprising that, in our money-obsessed society, the pursuit of money is offered as 'meaning' enough on its own. Through celebrity culture, and the celebration of entrepreneurs or the rich, we are encouraged to satisfy ourselves by consuming as much as possible. Few other goals are held up as worthwhile objectives for living. Yet given a choice, would we truly prefer to live in world with more stuff, or in one with more joy and better relationships? In a world of limited resources, we can't all have an oversized portion of the Cake - the sums simply do not add up. Yet bombarded with advertising and the ideal of the lifestyles of the super-rich, it's easy to oscillate between striving for the fantasy of wealth, and boredom or apathy. It is no wonder that, as the authors of *The Spirit Level* show, more unequal societies experience more anxiety, and more health and social problems.

How can it be the point of our existence to be born, work efficiently for the machine of economic growth, and then to die again? Surely life should be more than the sum of our economic contribution? As the Bishop of New York, the Rev Mark S. Sisk said during the 2011 *Occupy* protests:

> 'There can be little doubt that capitalism is a productive way to order economic life. But we need to remember... that that is all that it is. ...Capitalism is of no help at all in determining what is morally good—that is something that must instead be

determined by the community's wider values. And there should be no question that when an economic system fails to reflect those communal values, it should be modified and governed until it does.[368]

We need some wealth to survive, to eat and to shelter us; to meet our basic needs. Beyond that, our wealth has very little correlation to our happiness. Instead of having high levels of wealth, it is healthier to have good friends and new experiences, to work less and have more leisure time, to have more freedom to choose how to live, to spend more time with the kids, learn new skills, write books, make music, play sport, and learn a new language, or how to fix a bicycle. How much would you sacrifice to be able to live like that? Maybe rather than the endless pursuit of efficiency, we need to deliberately foster inefficiency; what else are hobbies, or cultural pursuits, or a lie-in, or bedtime stories?

By searching for meaning, and by changing what our goals and aims are as a society, we can begin to imagine a future for our country that is more reflective of the breadth and richness of the human experience. By changing the measure of our success from just our monetary or consumptive wealth to a wider definition of human and Earth wellbeing, it is possible for us to envisage a sustainable, happier, and more prosperous future.

TIME

THROUGH THE MORE EQUITABLE distribution of resources, it is more than possible for the people of the UK to enjoy higher levels of wellbeing. The apparently poor financial state of the country, (the supposed justification for the austerity narrative), is not supported by the unfolding evidence. This means that there is no reason why we cannot also afford to pursue more sustainable policies, whether in energy, transport, or elsewhere, to begin to reduce the impact that we have on the environment. There are hundreds of books, pamphlets, policy notes, and news articles written about the green infrastructure policy options available to us and their costs and effects, and it is not my intention to try and repeat any of that work in great detail here.[369] Some, such as green taxes, would raise additional revenue; others such as carbon quotas are effectively 'revenue neutral'. Others, such as investment in more sustainable infrastructure would obviously come at significant expense, yet are not beyond comparability with the choices we already make to develop less-green alternatives.

For example, widening roads and motorways is grossly expensive, at tens of millions of pounds per mile for the latter, yet proposals to fully integrate rapid coach travel into the motorway system would reduce CO_2 emissions per passenger by 85%, increase the carrying capacity of motorways tenfold, and cost a quarter of the price.[370, 371] The HS2 rail link, often billed as a green project but one that in reality will do virtually nothing to reduce the UK's carbon emissions, will have cost over £35bn by the time it is delivered in 2032, or roughly £1.8bn a year.[372] This is the same cost as a 60% increase in the number of UK bus routes, the most energy-efficient form of mass transport, or the same as a national roll-out of fibre-optic cable, which would transform the UK's digital infrastructure and make many journeys for business purposes unnecessary.[373, 374] It is also enough to build 50,000 affordable, energy-efficient homes, around half of the number that a recent National Housing Federation report found were needed annually, and in the process create 140,000 new jobs.[375] By contrast, our large defence projects including the replacement for the Trident nuclear missile system and new aircraft carriers could cost a whopping £130bn by 2030, whilst by some estimates the war in Afghanistan has cost the UK £37bn.[376] Sustainable policies are not only affordable in the short term, but make economic sense over the long term. An example is the 2006 government-commissioned Stern Review into the economics of climate change that, although now dated, showed that we could act to avoid the worst impacts of climate change for just 1% of global GDP a year, while failure to act could cost between 5% and 20% of GDP annually.[377]

Improvements in technology and infrastructure, if applied correctly, could be important tools in living more sustainably. However, changing our technology alone will not save us. We must remove the imperatives to growth by changing our financial system, and we must move away from our addiction to consumption and start to measure our success and development not by how much stuff we use up, but by our happiness and wellbeing. A further key element of living sustainably, and perhaps one of the most radical, is working less.

In earlier chapters we explored the 'efficiency imperative' for growth: how increasing productive efficiency requires an increase in the production and consumption of goods and services in order to keep the same number of people employed. However, as sustainable economies require a reduction, rather than increase in consumption, it will be necessary for us to reduce employment. The problem arises when this reduced amount of work is distributed unequally; some people work at full capacity, whilst others are completely unemployed. This creates significant social and economic issues. It is therefore just as important to distribute work equally as it is to distribute wealth equally. We must reduce our working hours and shorten our working week, and we must share what paid work that there is between us. This will have to happen a bit at a time, and it is difficult to tell at this stage how much less we should work; intuitively a move to somewhere between three and four days a week feels adequate to start with, but the New Economic Foundation's twenty-one hour working week proposal could be a longer-term goal.[378]

We examined this idea in earlier chapters as an economic argument. However, a shorter working week helps to support other aspects of our sustainable future: namely moving our measures of success from consumption to wellbeing, by focusing on what it is that brings us true happiness, and what it is that enables humanity to truly flourish. On these measures, the benefits of working less are extensive, and it's quite possible that we won't fully realise all that this enables us to do and how it transforms our lives until we actually try it.

Working less would lower our stress levels by allowing us to be less rushed in how we go about the tasks that we do. We would have more time for leisure, recreation, and exercise; we would be fitter and healthier. If we really were to move to a three-day working week then we would effectively be doubling the length of our weekend, every single week. Rather than squeezing the time we have with our children into a few minutes at the beginning and end of the day, with a bit of bonus time on the weekend, we would be able to give far more of our time to them – and of a much higher quality, when we are not tired and grumpy. This in turn could help reduce the issues associated with children not having enough time with their parents, or being left to be 'educated by the TV', or tablet computer.[379]

More free time would enable the improvement of gender relations and equality, as with fewer families under constant time pressures, and with work shared more equally, women would be able to pursue their careers to just the same extent as men. In the same way, men would have more time to truly support and care for their family. It's not a coincidence that one of the most common regrets of the dying, and especially for men, is that they worked too much.[380] Working less would provide more time for us to pursue our hobbies and learn new skills, take time to appreciate the world around us, to give more of our time for free, and pursue the other things that make up the *keys for happier living*. We would have more time to participate in local activities, build community and relationships, and so develop social resilience. This is a pressing social need considering the 800,000 older people and over 1.6million younger people that experience regular loneliness: a condition that can significantly damage physical and mental health.[381, 382]

Working less would have economic benefits too, although it is not always necessary to describe them as such, as they are first and foremost improvements to individual and social wellbeing. The stress reduction from working less, and the health gains associated with more time to exercise would go a long way to reducing the country's annual health bill, which currently includes £2bn a year for treating stress,[383] £14bn a year for diabetes (closely linked to obesity),[384] and £9bn for the treatment of heart disease.[385] Sharing employment around would significantly reduce costs on the welfare system, which would enable anyone to be in work that wanted to be. In addition, the whole country would benefit from improved levels of education, by affording people more time to learn and go back to college and university. People would be able to acquire further skills in their areas of interest, and so would be more likely to find work in a field that gave them satisfaction.

Finally, more free time and more evenly-distributed paid and unpaid work would enable us to move the provision of more of what we need in life from the economically definable 'market' to our families, friends, neighbours and communities. This is often a more environmentally sustainable approach, and would allow us to value things according to their contribution to communal and societal wellbeing, rather than by how much money they generate in an unsustainable financial system. This kind of thinking is demonstrated by a 2009 New Economics Foundation report that showed how hospital cleaners and waste-recycling workers are worth more to society than bankers and advertising executives.[386]

Food production is a good example. Our current energy-intensive agriculture system accounts for 24% of global CO_2 emissions, and 70% of all freshwater use. We now use *twenty times* more fossil fuel energy to produce a single calorie of food energy than in 1940, when we used more labour-intensive methods and less artificial fertiliser.[387] Growing our own food and putting the local infrastructure in place to allow for people to meet some of their nutritional needs themselves would help reduce carbon emissions in food production. Incidentally, it would also reduce our national GDP figures. This same pattern could be applicable to anything from repairing bicycles, clothes, and cars, to erecting fences or building houses. Taking the time to learn how to do things ourselves in more labour-intensive ways, instead of buying them from the market in a way that adds to GDP figures, would lead to a significant reduction in our environmental impact. It would also improve our wellbeing and happiness through acquiring new skills and strengthening social connections and infrastructure.

When we look at activities in this way and recognise the environmental and wellbeing benefits of seeking community solutions, rather than market solutions, to the things that we need, it becomes apparent how defunct GDP is as a measure of any kind of human progress. As David Korten outlines:

'The more environmentally burdensome ways of meeting a given need are generally those that contribute most to the GDP. For example, driving a mile in a car contributes more to GDP than riding a mile on a bicycle. Turning on an air conditioner adds more to GDP than opening a window. Relying on processed packaged food adds more than using natural foods purchased in bulk in reusable containers. We might say that GDP, technically a measure of the rate at which money is flowing through the economy, might also be described as a measure of the rate at which we are turning resources into garbage'.[388]

Author and environmental activist Vandana Shiva expands on this view:

'..."growth" measures the conversion of nature into cash, and commons into commodities. Thus nature's amazing cycles of renewal of water and nutrients are defined into nonproduction. The peasants of the world, who provide 72% of the food, do not produce; women who farm or do most of the housework do not fit this paradigm of growth either. A living forest does not contribute to growth, but when trees are cut down and sold as timber, we have growth. Healthy societies and communities do not contribute to growth, but disease creates growth through, for example, the sale of patented medicine'.[389]

Seeking non-market solutions to our needs also strengthens societal resilience in two important ways. At the moment we invest a high proportion of our waking hours into working to earn enough money to purchase the things that we need from the market. This works as long as we are well enough or we earn enough to be able to provide for ourselves and our families. However, as soon as things go wrong and we lose our jobs or fall ill, we are reliant on our money reserves to keep us ticking over. If we don't have this kind of financial backup then we can quickly get into difficulty and, although the state provides some limited financial support, this provides little more than a meagre existence. Yet by working less and moving away from market provision to community provision of services, a sudden drop in income does not have the same destructive impact. Instead the network of relationships that form community, and that we will have had the time to nourish and develop, can help us keep our heads above water.

Secondly, societal resilience is strengthened by shortening the route of goods and services through the economy. Our vast, over-extended, globalised supply networks for everything from food and fuel to washing machines and kitchen cabinets is vulnerable to fuel price fluctuations, natural disasters, political instability, and economic shocks, which are only going to become more frequent and extreme as our environment breaks down. A more communal provision of goods and services shortens supply lines, and encourages a mixed production of essential items at a more local level.

We are presented with a stark choice. We can keep our economic and financial systems as they are, work too hard and for too long, try and fulfil our need for a satisfying life through massive, unsatisfying consumption, and in the process completely overwhelm the capacity of the planet to sustain us, with disastrous consequences. Or, we can change our economic and financial systems, and share reducing amounts of consumption and work more equitably. We can work less, and fulfil our need for a satisfying life through the means that the wisest humans throughout history have shown us to be most satisfying: through taking time to build relationships, learn new skills, and appreciate what we have; to be happy with enough. Along the way we can reap the benefits of better health and wellbeing, invest into our children with our time and our energy, and pass onto them a prosperous future, living within a sustainable system on a flourishing Earth.

A GOOD LIFE

As HUMAN CIVILISATION has developed, and our endeavour has brought spectacular advancements in almost every field, it appears as though much of humanity, (especially those of us in developed countries), has forgotten or lost sight of what all of that endeavour was built upon. We forgot that it is the capacity of the Earth to sustain life that enables humanity to exist and flourish. Over the last fifty years humanity has been rediscovering this connection, and has attempted to engage with the challenge of how we can live sustainably on a finite planet. The field of environmental science has given us the understanding, as well as the raw data of this troubled relationship, and yet we have struggled to turn this knowledge into action. We have found obstacles at every stage: from the inertia of neoliberal globalisation, to inequality, vested interests, and our economic and financial systems. We have also had to explore our position in a society and culture dominated by the pursuit of money. Compared to the breadth and richness of the human experience, the ideals of our consumption culture offer barely a veneer of existence, yet it can sometimes feel overwhelming to question the accepted wisdoms and scratch just that little bit deeper.

And yet scratch we must. There are very real and very immediate limits to our existence on this Earth, and it is becoming increasingly apparent that we cannot impose an unlimited system on a finite planet. The system must be changed, and we have seen that logical, simple steps can be taken to alter our financial system so that we can live within limits without triggering continual, devastating crises. Yet giving ourselves the opportunity to live in harmony with our environment is only the beginning. Undertaking the task of transforming our economy and society along sustainable lines is more challenging, and requires not just a redesign of the way our system allocates wealth, but a change in our understanding of the nature of prosperity. This also causes us to ask questions of ourselves and of human nature, and requires us to look beyond economics and politics, and consider the purpose or 'meaning of life', whether we ultimately believe in one or not.

It is not enough for all of us to simply seek our own path. We are all deeply interconnected in more ways than we could possibly trace or understand. There is no absolute freedom; we are the products of forces beyond our control and even our lifetimes. The individual decisions that we make have consequences for the lives of people we will never meet, in places that we will never see, during years that we will never experience. And yet a great deal of modern economic and political thought operates entirely on the basis that we are isolated individuals making inherently selfish decisions, with no broader consideration beyond ourselves. Whilst this may be true for some people some of the time, it is not a philosophy on which to construct a framework for human civilisation. Life is too complex to separate out the economic sphere from the environmental, political, social, or individual; they are all intertwined and cannot be unpicked, and the values of one leak into the other. These values ultimately reflect our worldview and help us shape our future. We don't know what that future will look like exactly, or how much of it we'll even live to see, but the beliefs found in neoliberalism, and the wellbeing-based values expounded in this book clearly take us in two very different directions.

If we follow a neoliberal view that says we are inherently selfish animals, who will only ever behave in our own interests, and should be left to fend for ourselves in a survival-of-the-fittest, dog-eat-dog world, then what on Earth is our future going to look like? Would we want to leave that future to our children? Alternately, if we believe that we are human, with all the freedom of choice that that entails, including the choice to be selfless, to cooperate, to build community, to look after one another, to live sustainably within the capacity of the Earth, and value these above increasing consumption, then the future will look very different. Which one of these futures would we rather live in? Which one of these better describes the path of human evolution? Which one takes us forward and which takes us back? Whether we notice it or not, the beliefs and values we hold are actively shaping the world our children and grandchildren will inhabit.

It is good to have big ideas, to have beliefs, to search out meaning in life, and to express that with the fullness of our humanity, not just our spending habits. We are not just data on an economist's spreadsheet. There are few more depressing theories than the one that says we should not intervene, and that leaving the 'free' market to its own devices is best for everybody. Every human system operates within created rules that produce conditions that are better for some people than for others. The free market isn't some organic body that keeps itself in perfect condition if left alone: in its current configuration it is a feverish patient constantly fluctuating between unmanageable extremes of hot and cold. It produces huge disparities in wealth between the rich and poor, with the wealthy growing richer and the poor even poorer, excluded and exploited, along with all the accompanying social, cultural, and economic ills that this entails. The corporate capture of politics, and the power it affords those with money, undermines democracy and produces a rule of the wealthy for the benefit of the few at the expense of the many. It does all this while at the same time driving headlong, at great speed, towards ecological disaster. As a result, not intervening in the market and in our financial systems is as much a deliberate choice as any other. If we don't want this situation to change then by all means we should not intervene. If, however, we can imagine a better world, and we want ourselves and our children to live on a planet and in societies that are sustainable, just, and fair, then we have a right and an obligation to be courageous and change it to conform to the values that we hold.

We will not be alone in this. Many of us inherently feel that something is not as it should be, and there is a growing momentum behind sustainable, transformative ideas that seek to reconnect us with our humanity, of which this book presents just a small sample. At their core, these ideas involve us throwing out the old ideologies and the perceived wisdoms that have got us into this mess in the first place.

We have found that the apparently self-evident ideology of the 'free' market is anything but self-evident. Similarly, we have found that there is nothing natural about the way that money is created in our economy; it privatises the profit earned on what is a public good, whilst society is burdened with the corresponding debt and the risk that accompanies it. There are similar ideologies around the size and role of government and the amount of regulation it establishes. Yet there is no 'right' size for government, and there is no 'right' amount of regulation. It does not follow that smaller and less is better, any more than it follows that bigger and more is better. The right size of government is the size that creates a country in which we can all live well and be happy; the right amount of regulation is the amount that draws fairly the boundaries and limits that enable us to live within the sustainable capacity of the Earth. Likewise, there is no natural law that decides that the 'private' sector is good and the 'public' sector bad. Not only are the terms ill-defined and the line between them completely arbitrary and constantly moving, but there is no rule that the private sector allocates resources any more or less efficiently than the public sector.[390, 391] They are both capable of the efficient use of resources, and they are both capable of using them inefficiently.[392]

There is one natural law we can be sure of, however: we cannot have infinite on a finite planet. Despite the orientation of our economies to the contrary, more and more wealth is not good for us or the Earth. The race to increase wealth as production and consumption is a race to environmental calamity. On a national level, more important than how much wealth exists is how it's distributed, with unequal distributions leading to far lower levels of wellbeing and greater incidence of social issues. Our society may appear desensitised to both the level of inequality we face and the problems it causes. Yet when asked, most people want to live in a far more equal society than we do today, and the majority of people would welcome real wealth

distribution policies, such as higher taxes on the wealthiest, that would bring this more equal society about.[393]

The final perceived wisdom is that efficiency is always good, yet this does not stand up either economically or environmentally. Whilst efficiency has been useful at prior stages of human development, we are already a long way past the point when we need any more efficiency to sustain the entire human population in comfort. Environmentally, and in the absence of suitable restrictions and regulations, increases in efficiency actually lead to increases in the amount of resources used, and make it easier for us to more rapidly overwhelm planetary systems.[394] Efficiency also becomes economically self-defeating unless the benefits are shared in the form of more equal wages and less labour. There is an argument that both environmentally and economically we could do with less efficiency, rather than more of it. This is certainly the case on an individual level, too. What else are relationships, community, hobbies, culture, savouring the moment, and indulgent fun, other than the inefficient and economically unproductive allocation of time and resources?

We are emerging from a world where most discussions on the means and the ends of human progress revolve around money. Because of this, we have become used to seeing economics as the primary justification for achieving almost anything as a society or country.[395] We do not have to look very far to find examples of the atrocious treatment of people all over the globe defended in the name of economic progress. In the last few years the ideology behind austerity has brought this home to wealthy, developed countries in a very real way. Yet the economic argument should not be used as an excuse any longer. Britain is a vastly wealthy country, indeed one of the wealthiest in the world, and by distributing that wealth more equitably, and bringing money creation back under public control, there is no reason why we cannot shape our economy in a way that serves the needs of people, rather than the other way around.

What's more, economics cannot tell us how to live; it cannot tell us about the fullest expressions of our humanity, and what brings us the deepest happiness. Someone once said that economics would miss the incomprehensible wonders of human sex and simply note that the birth rate had gone up.[396] We must have some money to meet our basic needs, but to succumb to the advertisers and attempt to satisfy these needs through rampant consumerism is neither truly satisfying nor environmentally viable. As Alistair McIntosh puts it in *Hell and High Water*:

> 'The problem of consumerism comes about when the competitive pursuit of utility trashes the very means by which satisfaction might be derived – this is consumerism not as a passing stage of life, but as life retarded'.[397]

We have been conditioned to believe that there are no alternatives, yet our existing system is just another stage in history that is neither permanent nor inevitable. A sustainable future is possible but it will require less consumption; we need not go hungry but by current measures we will be less 'wealthy', whether we like it or not. We have a choice between learning to live within limits now, or have them visited on us not many years hence in far less pleasant circumstances which, by that point, will be far beyond our control.

We needn't be afraid of this change. A sustainable future is a better one; individually, communally, and globally; socially, economically, and environmentally. Yet there is no future for unrestrained consumption and GDP growth, as Korten explains, only partly in jest:

'As we surmise that the ancient Egyptians measured themselves by the size of their pyramids, a future civilization may look back on our era and conclude that we measured our progress by the size of our garbage dumps'.[398]

The human experience is not about consumption. It is about joy, love, friends, discovery, art, great feats and challenges, hope, community, dreams, and collective endeavour. We do not remember what the GDP growth rate was in 1969, but we do remember that humans stood on the Moon. We have had a glimpse of a future we can get excited about, and there is no fundamental law, economic or otherwise, that says it cannot be obtained. Let's have fun making it happen.

To Do

1 Restructure our financial system (the power to create wealth should be used for the benefit of ALL, NOT just a few)

2 Reclaim our political system from the service of corporate/commercial interests.

3 Promote the EVEN distribution of work, wealth and time

4 Reconsider the ways in which we measure prosperity:
AWAY FROM consumption (quantitative & unsustainable)
TOWARDS wellbeing (qualitative & sustainable)

5 Enjoy life:
explore & discover
learn
create
share - nurture generosity
be a positive influence
make friends!

ENDNOTES

1   Details of the IPCC reports can be found on the IPCC website, at http://www.ipcc.ch. The reports collect and analyse the latest scientific evidence on climate change every six years (the latest report summarised 6,000 peer-reviewed articles), and make projections based on this data. The latest report (AR5) is due out in full in 2014, although the advanced summary report was released in September 2013.

2   John Cook, Climate Communication Fellow for the Global Change Institute at the University of Queensland researches the level of consensus on climate issues. He ran the 2013 Consensus Project, and a summary of his research can be found on his website http://www.skepticalscience.com

3   BBC World Service Poll, conducted by *Globescan*, published 22nd May 2013

4   Polly Toynbee, 'This lost generation will cost us more than the cuts save', *Guardian,* 2nd July 2012

5   Charlotte McDonald-Gibson, 'A lost generation: Europe's unemployed youths face years trapped in downward spiral of poverty and exclusion', *Independent, 27*[th] June 2013

6   John Harris, 'The Tories are creating a hostile environment – not just for migrants', *Guardian, 13*[th] October 2013

7   There's a good, brief description of neoliberalism in the Introduction to *The Courageous State, by Richard Murphy (Searching Finance, London 2011). It is also sometimes inter-changed with the term 'free-market capitalism', or for the academics, 'laissez-faire capitalism'.*

8   Ha-Joon Chang, *23 Things They Don't Tell You about Capitalism*, *Allen Lane*, London 2010:3

9   In H. Jarrett (ed.), *Environmental Quality in a Growing Economy, MD: Resources for the Future/Johns Hopkins University Press, Baltimore 1966: 3-14*

10   Stephen Emmott, *10 Billion, Penguin Books, London 2013*

11   Rebecca Morelle, 'Rise in violence linked to climate change', *BBC News*, 2nd August 2013, http://www.bbc.co.uk/news/science-environment-23538771

12   John M. Broder, 'Climate change seen as threat to US security', *New York Times*, 8th August 2009

13   Gwynne Dyer, *Climate Wars, Oneworld, Oxford 2010:xiv*

14   BBC News, 'Scientists call for action to tackle CO_2 levels', 11th May 2013, http://www.bbc.co.uk/news/science-environment-22491491

15   Gwynne Dyer, *Climate Wars, Oneworld, Oxford 2010:61*

16   Tim Jackson, *Prosperity without Growth, Earthscan, London 2009:12*

17   http://350.org/en

18   Duncan Clark and Carbon Brief, 'The ultimate Climate Change FAQ', *Guardian*, 16th January 2012 http://www.guardian.co.uk/environment/series/the-ultimate-climate-change-faq

19   Alastair McIntosh, *Hell and High Water, Birlinn 2008:23*

20   NSIDC, 'Arctic sea ice extent settles at record seasonal minimum', *National Snow and Ice Data Centre*, 19th September 2012, http://nsidc.org/arcticseaicenews/2012/09/arctic-sea-ice-extent-settles-at-record-seasonal-minimum/

21   Hannah Hoag, 'Arctic snow cover shows sharp decline', *Nature*, 31st October 2012, http://www.nature.com/news/arctic-snow-cover-shows-sharp-decline-1.11709

22   Nerilie J. Abram et.al (2013), 'Acceleration of snow melt in an Antarctic peninsula ice core during the 20th century', *Nature Geoscience*, vol. 6:404-411

23   Steve Connor, 'Vast methane 'plumes' seen in Arctic ocean as sea ice retreats', *Independent*, 13th December 2011

24   Gwynne Dyer, *Climate Wars, Oneworld, Oxford 2010:92-93*

25 AMAP, AMAP Arctic Ocean Acidification Assessment: Key Findings, *Arctic Monitoring and Assessment Programme (AMAP), Oslo 2013*

26 Dan Laffoley et.al, The State of the Ocean 2013: Perils, Prognosis, and Proposals, *International Programme on the State of the Ocean, London 2013*

27 IPCC, 4th Assessment Report: Summary for Policy Makers, *International Panel on Climate Change, Valencia 2007:12*

28 Aslak Grinsted (2012), 'Projected Atlantic hurricane surge threat from rising temperatures', *Proceedings of the National Academy of Sciences of the United States (PNAS), vol. 110:14*

29 Pallab Ghosh, 'Prof Sir John Beddington warns of floods, droughts, and storms', *BBC News*, 25th March 2013, http://www.bbc.co.uk/news/science-environment-21357520

30 Professor John Sweeney, speaking to Kim Bielenberg, in 'We face cold future as jet stream goes south', *Irish Independent*, 25th May 2013

31   Gwynne Dyer, *Climate Wars, Oneworld, Oxford 2010:48*

32 Suzanne Goldenberg, 'Drought-damaged states face poor outlook as dry weather persists', *Guardian*, 10th January 2013

33 NCADAC, 'Federal Advisory Committee Draft Climate Assessment', *National Climate Assessment Development Advisory Committee, Washington 2013*

34 Brandon Keim, 'Record Arctic snow loss may be prolonging North American drought', *Wired Magazine*, 26th September 2012

35 BBC News, 'Britain's wheat crop down by a third after extreme weather', *BBC News*, 12th June 2013, http://www.bbc.co.uk/news/uk-22866982

36 Potsdam Institute for Climate Impact Research and Climate Analytics, 'Turn down the heat: climate extremes, regional impacts, and the case for resilience', *The World Bank, Washington 2013*

37 Prof Piers Forster et.al, 'Food security: Near future projections of the impact of drought in Asia', *Centre for Low Carbon Futures, Leeds 2012*

38 George Monbiot, 'Hunger Games', *Guardian*, 14th August 2012

39   John Vidal, 'Climate change: how a warming world is a threat to our food supplies', *Observer,* 13th April 2013

40   Orazio Attanasio et.al (2013), 'Welfare consequences of food price increases: evidence from rural Mexico', *Journal of Development Economics, vol.104:136-151*

41   Gwynne Dyer, *Climate Wars, Oneworld, Oxford 2010*

42   Stephen Emmott, *10 Billion, Penguin, London 2013:127*

43   Julie Brigham-Grette et.al (2013), 'Pliocene warmth, polar amplification, and stepped Pleistocene cooling recorded in NE Arctic Russia', Science, vol.340(6139):1421-1427

44   James Lovelock, 'The Earth is about to catch a morbid fever that may last as long as 100,000 years', *Independent,* 16th January 2006

45   BBC, *Stephen Fry in America, 2008, Episode 6, 50:00,* http://www.bbc.co.uk/programmes/b00flx59

46   George Monbiot, *'Breach of Trust',* 24th October 2013, http://www.monbiot.com/2013/10/24/breach-of-trust/

47   Richard Black, 'UN panel aims for a future worth choosing', *BBC News, 30th January 2012,* http://www.bbc.co.uk/news/science-environment-16775264

48   FOE Briefing Note, 'The government's green record', *Friends of the Earth, 20th April 2012,* http://www.foe.co.uk/resource/media_briefing/gvt_green_record.pdf

49   Poll for Greenpeace by YouGov, 19th March 2012, http://www.greenpeace.org.uk/media/reports/greenest-government-yougov-survey-results

50   Nicholas Watt, 'David Cameron pledges to reverse 'green charges' on energy bills', *Guardian,* 23rd October 2013

51   UK Government, 'Shale gas: government unveils plan to kick start investment with generous new tax breaks', *HM Treasury and Department for Communities and Local Government,* 19th July 2013, found at https://www.gov.uk/government/news/shale-gas-government-unveils-plan-to-kick-start-investment-with-generous-new-tax-breaks

52   http://www.sd-commission.org.uk

53   George Monbiot, 'Struck Dumb', *Guardian*, 6th November 2012

54   Roger Harrabin, 'Climate compensation row at Doha', *BBC News*, 5th December 2012, http://www.bbc.co.uk/news/science-environment-20613915

55   Alvin Toffler, *Futureshock, The Bodley Head, London 1970*

56   Juliette Jowit, 'Nuclear power: ministers offer reactor deal until 2050', *Guardian*, 18th February 2013

57   George Monbiot, 'Secrets of the Rich', *Guardian*, 19th February 2013

58   Carbon Tracker Initiative, 'Unburnable Carbon 2013: wasted capital and stranded assets', *Grantham Research Institute on Climate Change and the Environment, LSE, 2013*

59   If you only have five minutes, take a quick read of this summary of a recent composite report from the UN World Meteorological Organisation: http://www.wmo.int/pages/mediacentre/press_releases/pr_976_en.html

60   Craig S. Altemose et.al, 'Politicians and their professors: the discrepancy between climate science and climate policy', *Better Future Project, Cambridge MA 2012*

61   Gwynne Dyer, *Climate Wars,* Oneworld, Oxford 2010:xii

62   Griffin Carpenter, 'Model Behaviour: comparing climate science with economic forecasts', *New Economics Foundation, London 2014*

63   Alastair McIntosh, *Hell and High Water, Birlinn 2008:38*

64   Brad Plumer, 'Global CO2 emissions rising faster than worst-case scenarios', *Washington Post, 11th April 2011*

65   Ha-Joon Chang, 'There's a new jobs crisis – we need to focus on the quality of life at work', *Guardian*, 22nd December 2013

66   Andy Beckett, 'What is the 'Global Race'?', *Guardian, 22nd* September 2013

67   David Cameron, 'Prime Ministers speech to CBI', *Prime Minister's Office, 19th* November 2012

68   James Meadway, 'OBR forecasts only show the future Osborne wants to see', *New Economics Foundation, 5th* December

2012, http://www.neweconomics.org/blog/2012/12/05/
obr-forecasts-only-show-the-future-osborne-wants-to-see

69 Robert Winnett, 'David Cameron: no end in sight for austerity',
    Telegraph, 18th July 2012

70 Joshua Harris et.al, 'The 2015-16 spending round: a briefing
    note to accompany the IfG/IFS press briefing on 7th June 2013',
    Institute for Government, 2013

71 George Monbiot, 'How sustainability became sustained growth',
    Guardian, 22nd June 2012

72 George Monbiot, 'The Great Imposters', *Guardian, 7th August 2012*

73 Tony Judt, *Ill Fares the Land, Penguin, London 2010:39*

74 Mary Mellor, *The Future of Money, Pluto Press, London 2010:58*

75 This is purely a 'thought-experiment'. Should such an impos-
    sible scenario somehow play out in real life, the resulting events
    would be a lot more complicated!

76 By GDP per capita (constant yr2005 US$, EUROSTAT)

77 In adjusted net national income (constant yr2000 US$,
    EUROSTAT)

78 Based on data from the UNDP International Human
    Development Indicators, http://hdrstats.undp.org/en/indica-
    tors/66006.html

79 David C. Korten, When Corporations Rule the World,
    Kumarian Press, Connecticut 2001:53

80 Andrew Hood, *The Economic Circumstances of Cohorts Born
    between the 1940s and the 1970s, Institute for Fiscal Studies,
    London 2013*

81 Joe Earle, 'Is the recession over? These figures don't tell the
    whole story', *Guardian,* 11th May 2014

82 David Cameron, 'Plan for Britain's success: speech by the Prime
    Minister', *Prime Minister's Office, 10th June 2013*

83 Nouriel Roubini, Economist, interviewed for the film 'Inside
    Job'. Sony Pictures: 1:38:31.01

84 William C. Dudley et.al, 'How capital markets enhance
    economic performance and facilitate job creation', *Global
    Markets Institute: Goldman Sachs, 2004*

85 The regulation of the industry in the US was so lax that at the point immediately prior to the financial crisis, the risk management team of the Securities and Exchange Commission (SEC), the US regulator of the financial services industry, consisted of just one person.

86 Jing Luo et.al, 'CEO option compensation, risk-taking, and the financial crisis: evidence from the banking industry', *European Financial Management Association*, 2012

87 Mary Mellor, *The Future of Money, Pluto Press, London 2010:40-42*

88 Bill Thomas et.al, 'What caused the financial crisis?', *Wall Street Journal*, 27th January 2011

89 The full film can be watched here: http://www.filmsforaction.org/watch/inside_job_2010/

90 There are some clear graphs on this feature on the False Economy website: http://falseeconomy.org.uk/cure/what-is-the-deficit

91 Duncan Needham, 'Austerity Britain: it's déjà vu all over again, Cambridge University, 16th January 2013, http://www.cam.ac.uk/research/news/austerity-britain-its-d% C3%A9j%C3%A0-vu-all-over-again

92 Jim Pickard, 'Ed Balls outlines spending cuts and capital investment plans', *Financial Times*, 3rd June 2013

93 Office for National Statistics (ONS), *Public Sector Employment, Q4 2012*, 20th March 2013

94 The ONS data, as well as data from the Treasury and the Office for Budgetary Responsibility (OBR), is transformed into some useful graphs on the UK Public Spending website: http://www.ukpublicspending.co.uk/total_spending_2013UKbn

95 HM Treasury, *Public Expenditure Statistical Analyses 2012, July 2012*

96 CLASS, Austerity illusions and debt delusions, *Centre for Labour and Social Studies, London 2013*

97 Robert Skidelsky, 'Models behaving badly', *Project Syndicate, 18*[th] December 2012

98   Larry Elliot, 'George Osborne's deficit reduction plan: a blunt axe, blindly wielded', *Guardian*, 23rd September 2012

99   Philip Aldrick, 'No triple-dip for UK despite extra £75bn of debt, says CBI', *Telegraph*, 13th February 2013

100 Touchstone Blog, *'The UK economy unspun'*, http://touchstone-blog.org.uk/the-uk-economy-unspun

101 BBC News, 'Bank of England's Mark Carney warns on housing market', *BBC News*, 18th May 2014, http://www.bbc.co.uk/news/business-27459663

102 Richard Murphy, *Disappearing fast: the falling income of the UK's self-employed people, Tax Research, Downham Market 2013*

103 Nicholas Watt, 'Figures show huge rise in zero-hours contracts', *Guardian*, 10th March 2014

104 Office for National Statistics, *Statistical Bulletin: Labour Market Statistics, December 2013*, 18th December 2013

105 Emma Simpson, 'UK economy: underemployment on the rise', *BBC News*, 16th May 2012, http://www.bbc.co.uk/news/business-18091667

106 S Kirby et.al, 'Underemployment in the UK', *National Institute for Economic and Social Research*, 2nd May 2013, http://niesr.ac.uk/press/underemployment-uk-11285#.UjykfYakolT

107 Jonathan Cribb et.al, 'Living standards, poverty, and inequality in the UK: 2013', *Institute for Fiscal Studies, London 2013*

108 Graeme Wearden, 'Bank of England: no interest rate rises until unemployment drops to 7%', *Guardian*, 7th August 2013, http://www.theguardian.com/business/2013/aug/07/bank-of-england-forward-guidance-eurozone#block-52022425e4b0afb9dd11aa41

109 BBC News, 'Relate Survey: money problems causing family strain', 27th December 2012, http://www.bbc.co.uk/news/uk-20849015

110 Sarah Cassidy, 'Third of Graduates in low-skilled jobs – and they're the lucky ones', *Independent*, 7th March 2012

111 Angela Monaghan, 'No UK recovery until companies stop 'stashing the cash'', *Telegraph*, 14th April 2012

112 Tony Judt, *Ill Fares the Land, Penguin, London 2010:44*

113 Mary Mellor, *The Future of Money, Pluto Press, London 2010:127*

114 Richard Exell, 'Don't do that George', *Touchstone,* 11th September 2013, http://touchstoneblog.org.uk/2013/09/dont-do-that-george

115 Laura d'Andrea Tyson, 'Lessons on fiscal policy since the recession', *New York Times,* 3rd May 2013

116 The BBC 'Economy Tracker' tool has some clear visualisations: http://www.bbc.co.uk/news/10613201

117 The Trading Economics website aggregates and visualises a range of useful data: http://www.tradingeconomics.com/united-states/gdp-growth

118 Office for National Statistics, *Public Sector Finances bulletin, April 2013,* 22nd May 2013

119 HM Treasury, *Autumn Statement 2013, TSO, Norwich, December 2013*

120 The data on the national deficit is clearly visualised on the Guardian datablog website, here: http://www.guardian.co.uk/news/datablog/2010/oct/18/deficit-debt-government-borrowing-data#_

121 Data taken from HM Treasury and OBR, and visualised on the UK Public Spending website: http:/www.ukpublicspending.co.uk/spending_chart_1940_2013UKp_12c1li011mcn_Got

122 James Plunkett, 'The coalition's £11bn stealth cut', *New Statesman,* 21st September 2011

123 QE is explained well on the Bank of England website, which can be found here: http://www.bankofengland.co.uk/monetary-policy/pages/qe/default.aspx

124 Philip Inman, 'Yields on UK government bonds drop to record low at 1.87%', *Guardian,* 14th May 2012

125 Luke Thomas, 'The Cost of Kindness', *The Laboratory Canary,* 11th December 2013, http://laboratorycanary.blogspot.co.uk/2013/12/the-cost-of-kindness.html

126 Collins et.al, *Where Does Money Come From?, New Economics Foundation, London 2012*

127 Michael McLeay et.al, 'Money creation in the modern economy', Quarterly Bulletin 2014 Q1, Bank of England, London 2014, http://www.bankofengland.co.uk/publications/Documents/quarterlybulletin/2014/qb14q1prereleasemoneycreation.pdf

128 JK Galbraith, Money: Whence it came, Where it went, 1975

129 Andrew Jackson and Ben Dyson, Modernising Money, Positive Money 2012

130 Collins et.al, Where Does Money Come From?, New Economics Foundation, London 2012:11

131 RatingsDirect, Repeat after me: banks cannot and do not "lend out" reserves, Standard & Poor's Ratings Services, August 13th 2013 http://www.standardandpoors.com/spf/upload/Ratings_US/Repeat_After_Me_8_14_13.pdf

132 Mary Mellor, The Future of Money, Pluto Press, London 2010:50

133 Andrew Jackson and Ben Dyson, Modernising Money, Positive Money 2012:89

134 Aditya Chakrabortty, 'Don't be fooled by Richard Branson's defence of Virgin Trains', Guardian, 24th June 2013

135 Mary Mellor, The Future of Money, Pluto Press, London 2010:96

136 Bank for International Settlements (BIS), BIS Quarterly Review, March 2013, OTC derivatives table: found at http://www.bis.org/statistics/otcder/dt1920a.pdf

137 Ha-Joon Chang, 23 Things They Don't Tell You about Capitalism, Allen Lane, London 2010:238

138 Collins et.al, Where Does Money Come From?, New Economics Foundation, London 2012:117

139 Positive Money, 'How money creation by banks causes inflation', Accessed June 2013, at http://www.positivemoney.org/consequences/inflation/

140 Bain & Company Inc, 'A world awash with money: capital trends through 2020', http://www.bain.com/Images/BAIN_REPORT_A_world_awash_in_money.pdf

141 BBC News, 'Price of farmland trebles in less than a decade', 23rd August 2013 http://www.bbc.co.uk/news/business-23792583

142 Positive Money, 'The Positive Money system in plain English', *Positive Money, London 2012*

143 Philip Inman, 'Financial Services Authority chairman backs tax on 'socially useless' bank', *Guardian*, 27ᵗʰ August 2009

144 Murray Worthy, 'Broken markets: how financial market regulation can help prevent another global food crisis', *World Development Movement, September 2011*

145 Brandon Keim, 'Biofuels, speculation blamed for global food market weirdness', *Wired Magazine*, 5ᵗʰ October 2011

146 Daniel Prentzlin et.al, 'Farming money: how European banks and private finance profit from food speculation and land grabs', *Friends of the Earth Europe*, Brussels 2012

147 Andrew Jackson and Ben Dyson, *Modernising Money, Positive Money 2012:21*

148 Mervyn King, 'Banking: from Bagehot to Basel, and back again', speech at the *Buttonwood Gathering, New York*, 25ᵗʰ October 2010

149 Andrew Hough, 'City bonus row over 'sheer greed' of £14bn pay windfall', *Telegraph*, 20ᵗʰ July 2011

150 Collins et.al, *Where Does Money Come From?, New Economics Foundation, London 2012:95*

151 Ashley Seager et.al, 'Staring into the abyss', *Guardian*, 8ᵗʰ October 2008

152 Dominic Webb et.al, 'Government borrowing, debt and debt interest payments: historical statistics and forecasts', *House of Commons Library, Economic Policy and Statistics Section*, 13ᵗʰ March 2013

153 European Union, *Treaty on European Union (Consolidated Version), Treaty of Maastricht*, Maastricht 1992

154 Andrew Jackson and Ben Dyson, *Modernising Money, Positive Money 2012:14*

155 Collins et.al, *Where Does Money Come From?, New Economics Foundation, London 2012:80-83*

156 Alex Andreou, 'If you think you know what 'debt' is, read on', *Guardian, Monday 29ᵗʰ July, 2013*

157 Ambrose Evans-Pritchard, 'The Bank of England will never unwind QE, nor should it', *Telegraph, March 11th* 2014

158 Richard Murphy, 'UK state debt is not £1trillion – it is only £725billion', *Tax Research,* 25th January 2012, http://www.taxresearch.org.uk/Blog/2012/01/25/ uk-state-debt-is-not-1-trillion-it-is-only-725-billion

159 Collins et.al, *Where Does Money Come From?, New Economics Foundation, London* 2012:120

160 Collins et.al, *Where Does Money Come From?, New Economics Foundation, London* 2012:142

161 Collins et.al, *Where Does Money Come From?, New Economics Foundation, London* 2012:133

162 John Kay, 'The Power of the bond markets is a bluff waiting to be called, *Financial Times,* 10th September 2013

163 Andrew Jackson and Ben Dyson, *Modernising Money, Positive Money* 2012:170

164 Andrew Haldane, 'The $100billion question', comments at the Institute of Regulation & Risk, Hong Kong, 30 March 2010, found at http://www.bis.org/review/r100406d.pdf?frames=0

165 Tony Greenham et.al, 'Feather-bedding financial services: are British banks getting hidden subsidies?', *New Economics Foundation, London* 2011

166 Positive Money, 'Subsidising banks', found at http://www.positivemoney.org/consequences/subsidising-banks/

167 Andrew Jackson and Ben Dyson, *Modernising Money, Positive Money* 2012:170

168 Nicholas Shaxson and John Christensen, *The Finance Curse, Tax Justice Network, Chesham* 2013:48

169 Graeme Wearden, 'How the PPI scandal unfolded', *Guardian,* 5th May 2011

170 BBC News, 'Bank and card issuers face £1.3bn CPP compensation bill', http://www.bbc.co.uk/news/business-23791252

171 Jill Treanor, 'Lloyds Banking Group fined record £28m in new mis-selling scandal', *Guardian,* 12th December 2013

172 Craig Brown, 'HSBC pays £1.2 billion to settle US fraud probe', *Scotsman*, 11th December 2012

173 Robert Peston, 'Crackdown on Barclays Tax Schemes', *BBC News*, 28th February 2012, http://www.bbc.co.uk/news/business-17187277

174 BBC News, 'Timeline: LIBOR-fixing scandal', 6th February 2013, http://www.bbc.co.uk/news/business-18671255

175 'Day of reckoning as European banks' bill for misconduct mounts', *Financial Times*, 29th October 2013

176 Daniel Schäfer, 'Forex probes raise fears of a repeat of Libor scandal', *Financial Times*, 30th October 2013

177 Matt Taibbi, 'Everything is rigged: the biggest price-fixing scandal ever', *Rolling Stone*, 25th April 2013

178 Dyson et.al, *Towards a Twenty-First Century Banking and Monetary System: Submission to the Independent Commission on Banking, Centre for Banking, Finance and Sustainable Development*, 2010:19

179 Mary Mellor, *The Future of Money, Pluto Press, London* 2010:39

180 Andrew Jackson and Ben Dyson, *Modernising Money, Positive Money* 2012:143

181 Collins et.al, *Where Does Money Come From?, New Economics Foundation, London* 2012:110-112

182 Collins et.al, *Where Does Money Come From?, New Economics Foundation, London* 2012:143-145

183 Andrew Jackson and Ben Dyson, *Modernising Money, Positive Money, London* 2012

184 Positive Money, 'The Positive Money system in plain English', *Positive Money, London* 2012

185 Andrew Jackson and Ben Dyson, *Modernising Money, Positive Money* 2012:25

186 Positive Money, 'Bank of England (Creation of Currency) Bill', *a proposal from Positive Money*, 12th April 2013

187 Jaromir Benes et.al, 'The Chicago Plan revisited', *IMF Working Paper, International Monetary Fund, Washington D.C* 2012

188 Andrew Grice, 'Outgoing Bank of England Governor Sir
     Mervyn King accuses George Osborne of lobbying on behalf of
     banks to weaken regulation', *Telegraph*, 25th June 2013

189 Maeve McClenaghan, 'Big banks and thinktanks', *The Bureau of
     Investigative Journalism*, 12th July 2012

190 Nick Mathiason, 'Hedge funds, financiers and private equity
     make up 27% of Tory funding', *The Bureau of Investigative
     Journalism*, 30th September 2011

191 Collins et.al, *Where Does Money Come From?*, New Economics
     Foundation, London 2012:125

192 From my research, the origins of this phrase appear to be
     unknown. It does seem though to have been first popularised at
     pro-prohibition rallies in America in the late 19th Century

193 Mariana Mazzucato, *The Entrepreneurial State, Demos, London
     2011*

194 Polly Toynbee, 'Competition is killing the NHS, for no good
     reason but ideology', *Guardian*, 15th November 2013

195 Karen Davis et.al, *Mirror, Mirror on the Wall: how the perfor-
     mance of the US healthcare system compares internationally*, The
     Commonwealth Fund, June 2010

196 Zoe Williams, 'How to make recidivism and costs rise? Privatise
     probation', *Guardian*, 30th October 2013

197 Richard Murphy, 'The autumn statement announces increasing
     privatisation of HMRC', Tax Research, 5th December 2013,
     http://www.taxresearch.org.uk/Blog/2013/12/05/the-autumn-
     statement-announces-increasing-privatisation-of-hmrc/

198 Howard Hotson, 'Don't look to the ivy league', *London Review of
     Books, Vol 33, No 10, 19th* May 2011

199 Gwyn Topham, 'East coast rail pays out millions in dividends to
     taxpayers', *Guardian, 7th* October 2013

200 Simon Mundy et.al, 'Landlords in the driving seat at Southern
     Cross', *Financial Times, 19th* June 2011

201 Alex Preston, 'Southern Cross, a haunting example of how
     privatisation can go wrong', *New Statesman, 23rd* June 2011

202 HM Government, *Open Public Services White Paper, Cabinet
     Office, July 2011*

203 John Harris, 'Hinkley Point nuclear power station: a new type of nationalisation', *Guardian*, 21st October 2013

204 George Monbiot, 'Line of battle', 26th March 2013, http://www.monbiot.com/2013/03/25/line-of-battle/

205 John Harris, 'The Royal Mail sell-off plan is daylight robbery of our postal service', *Guardian*, 10th July 2013

206 Andrew Bowman et.al, *The Great Train Robbery: rail privatisation and after, Centre for Research on Socio-Cultural Change (CRESC), Manchester 2013*

207 Seumus Milne, 'The grip of privatisation on our vital services has to be broken', *Guardian*, 29th October 2013

208 Centre for Labour and Social Studies (CLASS), *Why inequality matters, My Fair London, London 2012*

209 Jonathan Cribb et.al, *Living standards, poverty, and inequality in the UK: 2012, Institute for Fiscal Studies, London 2012*

210 The Poverty Site has clear visualisations of the ONS data, found at http://www.poverty.org.uk/09/index.shtml

211 Sarah Dransfield, *A Tale of Two Britains: inequality in the UK, Oxfam, Oxford 2014*

212 Phillip Inman, 'Britain's richest 1% own as much as poorest 55% of population', *Guardian*, 15th May 2014

213 Her Majesty's Revenue and Customs (HMRC), UK Personal Wealth Statistics 2008 to 2010, *Office for National Statistics (ONS), 28th September 2012*

214 Agenda to the Methodist Conference, found at: http://www.methodistconference.org.ukmedia/41199/11-poverty-and-inequality-0511.pdf?dm_i=BVI,GV7 A,335PP2,1DKBL,1

215 OECD forum on tackling inequality, *Growing income inequality in OECD countries: what drives it and how can policy tackle it?, OECD, Paris 2nd May 2011*

216 Ricardo Fuentes-Nieva et.al, *Working for the few: political capture and economic inequality, Oxfam, Oxford 2014*

217 Herbert Marcuse, *One Dimensional Man, Beacon Press, Boston 1966*

218 Nicholas Shaxson, 'A tale of two Londons', *Vanity Fair, April 2013*

219 Nicholas Shaxson, 'A tale of two Londons', *Vanity Fair, April 2013*

220 Data taken from the US Census Bureau, 2011

221 Luisa Kroll, 'Inside the 2013 billionaires list: facts and figures', *Forbes Magazine*, 25th March 2013

222 Louise Gray, 'David Attenborough – Humans are plague on Earth', *Telegraph*, 22nd January 2013

223 George Monbiot, 'Enough Already', *Guardian*, 6th May 2013

224 Richard Murphy, *Secrecy Jurisdictions: Research Briefing, for the Financial Integrity and Economic Development Task Force, Tax Research, Downham Market 2010, found at* http://www.taxresearch.org.uk/Documents/Secrecyjurisdiction.pdf

225 Countries in the British 'web' features highly on the Financial Secrecy Index, found at: http://www.financialsecrecyindex.com/2011results.html

226 Just type 'tax planning' into google...

227 Austin Mitchell et.al, *The Pin-stripe mafia: how accounting firms destroy societies, Association for Accountancy and Business Affairs, Basildon 2011*

228 Nicholas Shaxson, *Treasure Islands, The Bodley Head, London 2011*

229 Maria Gonzalez et.al, 'Bankers on the Beach', *International Monetary Fund (IMF): Finance and Development, Vol 48, No 2, June 2011*

230 George Eaton, 'Osborne isn't increasing funding for HMRC – he's cutting it', *New Statesman*, 3rd December 2012

231 ARC President Graham Black, in evidence to the HOC Treasury Select Committee, Wednesday 29th June 2011

232 Vanessa Houlder, 'Revenue suffers big drop in yield from company probes', *Financial Times, September 8th 2013*

233 BBC News, 'HMRC 'loses nerve' chasing big firms, says MP', 19th December 2013, http://www.bbc.co.uk/news/business-25430826

234 Rajeev Syal, 'Britain's £35bn tax gap is 'tip of the iceberg', says Margaret Hodge, *Guardian*, 28th October 2013

235 Richard Murphy, 'HMRC's new tax gap report: a work of fiction and guess work', *Tax Research UK*, 11th October 2013, http://www.taxresearch.org.uk/Blog/2013/10/11/hmrcs-new-tax-gap-report-a-work-of-fiction-and-guess-work/

236 Rob Evans et.al, 'Big business disputes £25bn in tax – equivalent to a year's spending cuts', *Guardian*, 22nd June 2011

237 Larry Elliot et.al, *A green new deal, New Economics Foundation*, London 2008

238 Dev Kar et.al, *Illicit financial flows from developing countries: 2001-2010, Global Financial Integrity, Washington D.C.* 2012

239 OECD, 'Development: aid to developing countries falls because of global recession', available at: http://www.oecd.org/newsroom/developmentaidtodevelopingcountriesfallsbecauseofglobalrecession.htm

240 UNESCO, *EFA Global Monitoring Report 2012: Youth and Skills: putting education to work, UNESCO, Paris 2012*

241 Sharon Beder, *Suiting Themselves: how corporations drive the global agenda*, Earthscan, London 2006

242 Holly Watt et.al, 'Andrew Lansley bankrolled by private health-care provider', *The Telegraph*, 14th January 2010

243 An example is The Confederation of British Industry (CBI) for big businesses

244 Think tanks do not currently have to disclose their funding sources, although occasionally news emerges of who does fund them. It was recently disclosed that two significant libertarian think tanks receive funding from tobacco firms, and produce large amounts of pro-tobacco literature. See Jamie Doward, 'Health groups dismayed by news 'big tobacco' funded right-wing thinktanks', *The Observer*, 1st June 2013

245 Jonathan Ford, 'All carrot, no stick', *The Financial Times*, 22nd March 2013

246 Damien Carrington, 'Energy lobby insiders will lead cold war against Labour', *The Guardian*, 6th October 2013

247 Aditya Chakrabortty, 'David Milliband and debasement of British politics', *The Guardian*, 1st April 2013

248 Rajeev Syal et.al, 'Big Four accountants use knowledge of Treasury to help rich avoid tax', *The Guardian*, 26th April 2013

249 Gerri Peev, 'Conservative MP who chairs climate change committee earns £140k from green energy firms', *Daily Mail*, 13th August 2012

250 Nick Mathiason et.al, 'HSBC under fire over leading role in land deals for Mubarak regime', *The Observer*, 1st May 2011

251 John Harris, 'School surveillance: how big brother spies on pupils', *The Guardian*, 9th June 2011

252 The 2010 Browne Review of Higher Education, was led by Baron Browne of Madingley, former Chief Executive of BP, Chairman of Quadrilla Resources (a fracking company), and Managing Director of the investment company Riverstone Holdings LLP. Since 2001 he has also sat in the House of Lords.

253 Ian Davis is a non-executive Director of BP, Director of Johnson & Johnson, Chairman of Rolls Royce, former senior partner at McKinsey, and a non-executive member of the UK Government Cabinet Office.

254 Richard Murphy, 'KPMG cannot be put in charge of the hen house, let alone HMRC and financial regulation', *Tax Research UK*, 11th April 2013

255 All six current non-executive directors of HMRC have a current or past background in big business. See http://www.hmrc.gov.uk/governance/non-exec.htm

256 James Ball et.al, 'Buddy scheme to give more multinationals access to ministers', *The Guardian*, 18th January 2013

257 'Cash for access: Peter Cruddas bankrolled Chequers event', *The Telegraph*, 1st April 2012

258 Damian Carrington, 'Owen Paterson held urgent meeting for fracking boss, documents show', *The Guardian*, 21st March 2014

259 Toby Helm et.al, 'David Cameron told to sack strategy chief over link to tobacco giants', *The Observer*, 13th July 2013

260 George Monbiot, 'Why politics fails', 12th November 2013, http://www.monbiot.com/2013/11/11/why-politics-fails/

261 Andrew Robertson, 'NHS Privatisation: Compilation of financial and vested interests', Social Investigations, 18th February 2012, found at http://socialinvestigations.blogspot.co.uk/2012/02/nhs-privatisation-compilation-of.html

262 Andrew Robertson, 'The Telegraph, the think tank, and very dodgy business', Social Investigations, 2nd August 2012, found at http://socialinvestigations.blogspot.co.uk/2012/08/the-telegraph-think-tank-and-very-dodgy.html

263 Mehdi Hasan, 'We are not all in this together', New Statesman, 21st October 2010

264 Stephen Crone et.al, 'Just 50 donor groups have supplied over half of the Conservative party's declared donation income in the last decade', London School of Economics, 20th December 2010, found at http://blogs.lse.ac.uk/politicsandpolicy/archives/6272

265 The CBI initially campaigned against the introduction of the minimum wage in 1999, and then continued to campaign against further increases. See Victor Keegan, 'A rich complaint', Guardian, 28th September 2006

266 Tim Worstall, 'UK Uncut Unravelled', Institute for Economic Affairs, March 2011

267 David Smith, Restructuring the UK tax system: some dynamic considerations, Institute for Economic Affairs, March 2011

268 Nicholas Shaxson, Treasure Islands, The Bodley Head, London 2011

269 James Moore, 'HSBC in new threat to leave the UK over Osborne banking levy', Independent, 6th November 2010

270 Louise Armitstead et.al, 'Institute of Directors warns government not to wobble on austerity measures', Telegraph, 3rd December 2010

271 Mark Littlewood, 'The Hole we're in: the challenge for free-marketeers in 2010 and beyond', meeting of the Institute of Economic Affairs, 24th March 2010, found at: http://www.iea.org.uk/sites/default/files/publications/files/upldbook513pdf.pdf

272 Ed Holmes et.al, Controlling Public Spending: Pay, staffing and conditions in the public sector, *Policy Exchange, London 2010*

273 Jesse Drucker, 'OECD enables companies to avoid $100 billion in taxes', *Bloomberg, 18th* March 2013

274 The Transatlantic Trade and Investment Partnership is a scary global agreement, formulated almost entirely outside of the public (think democratic) eye. The Think-Left website has a good summary: http://think-left.org/2013/02/20/are-we-already-in-the-post-democratic-era/ as does George Monbiot, '*A global ban on left-wing politics*', 5th November 2013

275 John Kenneth Galbraith, *The Economics of Innocent Fraud*, Penguin, London 2009:38

276 Ha-Joon Chang, 23 *Things they don't tell you about Capitalism*, Allen Lane, London 2010:10

277 George Monbiot, 'With threats and bribes, Gove forces schools to accept his phoney 'freedom'', *Guardian, 4th* March 2013

278 BBC News 'Tim Yeo rejects committee coaching claim', 9th June 2013, found at http://www.bbc.co.uk/news/uk-politics-22830707

279 Georgia Graham, 'David Cameron accused of cronyism as Conservative donors join him on China trip', *Telegraph, 2nd* December 2013

280 George Monbiot, 'Transylvanian Count to Chair Bloodbank', 6th December 2013, http://www.monbiot.com/2013/12/06/transylvanian-count-to-chair-bloodbank/

281 Tim Shipman, 'The 'cronies' honours list: Controversy over knighthood for PR man who holidayed with Cameron and awards to Tory and LibDem donors', *The Daily Mail, 30th* December 2013

282 John Kenneth Galbraith, *The Economics of Innocent Fraud*, Penguin, London 2009:44

283 Patrick Wintour, 'The day Britain changes: welfare reforms and coalition cuts take effect', *Guardian, 1st* April 2013

284 Dominic Rossi, 'Companies must reinvest their cash hoard', *Financial Times, 27th* November 2013

285 Richard Murphy, 'Osborne's giving away £58 billion to big business over six years', *Tax Research UK, 21*st March 2013, found at http://www.taxresearch.org.uk/Blog/2013/03/21/osbornes-giving-away-58-billion-to-big-business-over-six-years/

286 Ha-Joon Chang, *23 Things They Don't Tell You about Capitalism, Allen Lane, London 2010:137*

287 David Cay Johnston, 'Billions of Tax Dollars Later, No New Jobs for New York', *TaxAnalysts.com,* 9th December 2013, http://www.taxanalysts.com/www/features.nsf/Articles/DC64E543F3D1B2DE85257C3C00530CB6?OpenDocument

288 Tom MacInnes et. al., *Monitoring policy and social exclusion 2013, Joseph Rowntree Foundation, York 2013*

289 Janet Lowe, *Warren Buffet Speaks: wit and wisdom of the world's greatest investor, John Wiley & Sons, Hoboken 1997:164-165*

290 Robin Harding et.al, 'Perils of austerity theory take centre stage', *Financial Times, 17*th April 2013

291 Paul Hawken, *YES! A Journal of Positive Futures*, Summer 1999:40

292 Nicholas Watt, 'David Cameron makes leaner state a permanent goal', *Guardian, 12*th November 2013

293 Stephen Reid, 'Mythbusters: Britain is broke – we can't afford to invest', *The New Economics Foundation, 4*th April 2013, found at http://www.neweconomics.org/blog/entry/mythbusters-britain-is-broke-we-cant-afford-to-invest

294 The BBC News 'economy tracker' has some good visualisations of the ONS data, found at http://www.bbc.co.uk/news/10604117

295 James Mirza-Davies, *Youth Unemployment Statistics, House of Commons Library, Economic Policy and Statistics section, 17*th July 2013

296 Lizzie Crowley et.al, *International Lessons: Youth unemployment in the global context, The Work Foundation, London 2013*

297 Regional Economic Analysis, changes in real earnings in the UK and London, *Real wages down 8.5% since 2009, Office for National Statistics, 5*th April 2013

298 Matthew Whittaker, *Squeezed Britain 2013, The Resolution Foundation, London 2013*

299 Howard Reed et.al, 'Where have all the wages gone?: lost pay and profits outside financial services', *Touchstone Extras, Trades Union Congress, London 2012*

300 James Plunkett et.al., *The State of Living Standards, Resolution Foundation, London 2014*

301 Steve Hawkes, 'Biggest drop in savings for 40 years, Bank of England figures reveal', *Telegraph,* 2nd December 2013

302 Matthew Whittaker, *Closer to the Edge?, The Resolution Foundation, London 2013*

303 Niall Cooper et.al, *Walking the breadline: the scandal of food poverty in 21st Century Britain, Oxfam, Oxford 2013*

304 Press Association, 'Red Cross to distribute food to Britain's poor and hungry', *Guardian,* 11th October 2013

305 Charlie Cooper, 'Food poverty in UK has reached level of 'public health emergency', warn experts', *Independent,* 4th December 2013

306 Dr Simon Duffy, *Counting the Cuts, The Centre for Welfare Reform, Sheffield 2014*

307 Christina Beatty et.al, *Hitting the poorest places hardest: the local and regional impact of welfare reform, Centre for Research Economic and Social Research, Sheffield Hallam University, April 2013*

308 The Financial Times, 'Austerity Audit', in-depth editorial found at http://ig.ft.com/austerity-audit/?ftcamp=crm/email/2013411/nbe/UKMorningHeadlines/product

309 Ben Martin, 'Cash reserves rise to £166bn as businesses play it safe', *Telegraph,* 16th September 2013

310 Peter Adamson, *Innocenti Report Card 11, child well-being in rich countries: a comparative overview, UNICEF, Florence 2013*

311 Peter Adamson, *Innocenti Report Card 11, child well-being in rich countries: a comparative overview, UNICEF, Florence 2013:4*

312 Donald Hirsch, *An estimate of the cost of child poverty in 2013, Centre for Research in Social Policy, Loughborough University, found at* http://www.donaldhirsch.com/costofpoverty.pdf

313 Richard Murphy et.al, *Green quantitative easing: paying for the economy we need, Finance for the Future, Downham Market 2010*

314 National Offender Management Service, *Information release: costs per place and costs per prisoner by individual prison, Ministry of Justice,* 27ᵗʰ October 2011

315 Martin Wolf, 'How austerity has failed', *New York Review of Books,* 11ᵗʰ July 2013

316 Andrew Haldane, 'The $100billion question', comments at the Institute of Regulation & Risk, Hong Kong, 30 March 2010, found at http://www.bis.org/review/r100406d.pdf?frames=0

317 Gerard Ryle et.al, 'Secret files expose offshore's global impact', *The International Consortium of Investigative Journalists,* 3ʳᵈ April 2013

318 Heather Stewart, 'Wealth doesn't trickle down - it just floods offshore, research reveals', *Observer,* 21ˢᵗ July 2012

319 Richard Murphy, 'HMRC are going to lose more than 6% of staff tackling tax avoidance and evasion in the next year', *Tax Research,* 7ᵗʰ February 2013, found at http://www.taxresearch.org.uk/Blog/2013/02/07/hmrc-are-going-to-lose-more-than-6-of-staff-tackling-tax-avoidance-and-evasion-in-the-next-year/

320 Information on the *General Anti-Tax Avoidance Principle Bill, can be found at* http://services.parliament.uk/bills/2012-13/generalantitaxavoidanceprinciple.html

321 George Monbiot, 'We have no right to our rivers while Richard Benyon's interests are served', *Guardian,* 4ᵗʰ April 2013

322 The Poverty Site has clear visualisations of the ONS data, found at http://www.poverty.org.uk/09/index.shtml

323 Patrick Collinson, 'Richest 10% of UK households own 40% of wealth, ONS says', *Guardian,* 3ʳᵈ December 2012

324 Jerry Jones, Land value for public benefit, *Labour Land Campaign, Dorset 2008*

325 George Monbiot, 'I agree with Churchill: let's get stuck into the real shirkers', *Guardian*, 21st January 2013

326 Jerry Jones, Land value for public benefit, *Labour Land Campaign*, Dorset 2008

327 George Monbiot, 'Line of Battle', *Guardian*, 26th March 2013

328 Jerry Jones, Land value for public benefit, *Labour Land Campaign*, Dorset 2008

329 Simon Jenkins, 'Unlike most government reforms, the impact of the planning changes is forever', *Guardian*, 27th March 2013

330 David Cooper, 'Why all progressives should support a land value tax', *New Statesman*, 18th February 2013

331 Jerry Jones, Land value for public benefit, *Labour Land Campaign*, Dorset 2008

332 Chris Giles et.al, 'UK Budget: no Plan B for the economy', *Financial Times*, 14th March 2013

333 Kwasi Kwarteng et.al, *Britannia Unchained: global lessons for growth and prosperity*, Palgrave Macmillan, London 2012

334 Richard Murphy, *The Courageous State, Searching Finance*, London 2011:30-31

335 Martin Wolf, 'Enslave the robots and free the poor', *Financial Times*, 11th February 2014

336 Paul Krugman, 'Robots and Robber Barons', *New York Times*, 9th December 2012

337 Howard Reed et.al, 'Where have all the wages gone?: lost pay and profits outside financial services', *Touchstone Extras, Trades Union Congress*, London 2012

338 Angela Monaghan, 'No UK recovery until companies stop 'stashing the cash'', *Telegraph*, 14th April 2012

339 Michael Foley, *The Age of Absurdity, Simon & Schuster, London* 2010:177

340 Anna Coote et.al, '21 Hours: why a shorter working week can help us all flourish in the 21st Century', *New Economics Foundation*, London 2010

341 Anna Coote, '21 Hours', New Economics Foundation, http://www.neweconomics.org/publications/entry/21-hours

342 Catherine Brahic, 'Humanity's carbon budget set at one trillion tonnes', *New Scientist*, 29th April 2009

343 Energy and Climate Change Committee, *Consumption Based Emissions Reporting: twelfth report of session 2010-2012, volume 1, the House of Commons*, 27th March 2012

344 George Monbiot, 'The Great Unmentionable', *Guardian*, 12th April 2013

345 George Monbiot, *Heat: How we can stop the planet burning*, Penguin, London 2007:61

346 Alastair McIntosh, *Hell and High Water*, Birlinn 2008: 91

347 Tim Jackson, *Prosperity without Growth*, Earthscan, London 2009:95

348 Richard Wilkinson and Kate Pickett, *The Spirit Level*, Penguin, London 2010:223

349 James Brown et.al, Energetic Limits to Economic Growth, *Bioscience, Vol 61, No 1, University of California Press, January 2011*

350 Tim Garrett, No way out? The double-bind in seeking global prosperity alongside mitigated climate change, *Earth System Dynamics, Vol 3*, 2012

351 Richard Wilkinson and Kate Pickett, *The Spirit Level*, Penguin, London 2010:223

352 GNP is a measure of production closely related to GDP

353 David C. Korten, When Corporations Rule the World, Kumarian Press, Connecticut 2001:44–45

354 Alastair McIntosh, *Hell and High Water*, Birlinn, Edinburgh 2008: 161

355 Tim Jackson, 'An Economic Reality Check', speech at *Technology, Entertainment, Design (TED), July 2010, available at:* http://www.ted.com/talks/tim_jackson_s_economic_reality_check.html

356 Richard Layard, *Happiness: Lessons from a New Science*, Penguin, London 2005

357 Richard Wilkinson and Kate Pickett, *The Spirit Level*, Penguin, London 2010

358 Richard Layard, *Happiness: Lessons from a New Science*, Penguin, London 2005:44

359 http://www.actionforhappiness.org/

360 Michael Foley, *The Age of Absurdity: why modern life makes it hard to be happy*, Simon and Schuster, London 2010

361 Found at: http://www.neweconomics.org/projects/entry/five-ways-to-well-being

362 Found at: http://www.actionforhappiness.org/10-keys-to-happier-living

363 George Monbiot, 'Hey, advertisers, leave our defenceless kids alone', *Guardian*, 15th April 2013

364 Andrew Simms and Ruth Potts, *The New Materialism*, Bread, Print, and Roses, London 2012

365 Andrew Simms and Ruth Potts, *The New Materialism*, Bread, Print, and Roses, London 2012:7

366 Michael Foley, *The Age of Absurdity: why modern life makes it hard to be happy*, Simon and Schuster, London 2010: 68

367 John Kenneth Galbraith, *The Economics of Innocent Fraud*, Penguin, London 2009:20

368 http://www.dioceseny.org/news_items/212-bp-sisk-writes-on-ows-and-capitalism

369 George Monbiot's *'Heat: How we can stop the planet burning' is a good place to start, as is the work of the Green New Deal group*, http://www.greennewdealgroup.org/

370 Juliette Jowit, 'M1 widening to cost £21m per mile', *Guardian*, 6th May 2007

371 George Monbiot, *Heat: How we can stop the planet burning*, Penguin, London 2007:150

372 Mark Odell et.al, 'HS2 cost rises £2bn in 12 months', *Financial Times*, 28th January 2013

373 Bus Statistics, *Annual Bus Statistics 2010/11, Department for Transport*, 20th October 2011, found at https://www.gov.uk/government/uploads/system/uploads/attachment_data/file/8963/busstats2010.pdf

374 Elliot et.al, A national plan for the UK: the fifth anniver-
sary report of the Green New Deal group, *Green New Deal
Group, 2013,* http://www.greennewdealgroup.org/wp-content/
uploads/2013/09/Green-New-Deal-5th-Anniversary.pdf

375 National Housing Federation, Spending Review 2013 -
Member Briefing, London 2013 http://www.housing.org.uk/
publications/browse/spending-review-briefing

376 Frank Ledwidge, *Investment in Blood, Yale Univeristy Press,
London 2013*

377 Nicholas Stern, *The economics of climate change: the Stern
review, Cambridge University Press, Cambridge 2006*

378 Anna Coote et.al, '21 Hours: why a shorter working week
can help us all flourish in the 21st Century', *New Economics
Foundation, London 2010*

379 James Meikle, 'Research links children's psychological problems
to prolonged screen time', *Guardian, Wednesday 28*[th] *August*
2013

380 Bronnie Ware, *The top five regrets of the dying, Hay House,
London 2011*

381 Research aggregated at *Campaign to End Loneliness,* http://
www.campaigntoendloneliness.org/threat-to-health/

382 Jo Griffin, *The Lonely Society, The Mental Health Foundation,
London 2010*

383 Roger Dobson, 'Stress due to mounting debt costs NHS
millions', *Telegraph, 25*[th] *October 2008*

384 Kanavos, van den Aardweg and Schurer. *Diabetes expenditure,
burden of disease and management in 5 EU countries, London
School of Economics, January 2012, sourced from* http://www.
diabetes.co.uk/cost-of-diabetes.html

385 British Heart Foundation, data sourced from http://www.bhf.
org.uk/research/heart-statistics/economic-costs.aspx

386 Ellis Lawler et.al, *A bit rich: calculating the real value to society of
different professions, New Economics Foundation, London 2009*

387 Nafeez Ahmed, 'Peak soil: industrial civilisation is on the verge
of eating itself', *Guardian, 7*[th] *June 2013*

388 David C. Korten, When Corporations Rule the World, Kumarian Press, Connecticut 2001:44

389 Vandana Shiva, 'How economic growth has become anti-life', *Guardian,* 1st November 2013

390 Stephen Reid, 'Mythbusters: the private sector is more efficient than the public sector', *New Economics Foundation,* 25th April 2013, found at http://www.neweconomics.org/blog/entry/mythbusters-the-private-sector-is-more-efficient-than-the-public-sector

391 Colin Leys, 'It's not just Mid Staffordshire. Private hospitals fail too', *Guardian,* 28th October 2013

392 Anyone who believes that it is a universal rule that the private sector stands for greater efficiency than the public sector should read Naomi Klein's *The Shock Doctrine, Penguin Books, London 2007*

393 Centre for Labour and Social Studies (CLASS), *Why inequality matters, My Fair London, London 2012*

394 Duncan Clark, 'Why we can't quit fossil fuels', *Guardian,* 17th April 2013

395 Peter Dominiczak, 'Maria Miller tells arts world to show how it is boosting the economy', *Telegraph,* 24th April 2013

396 I read a sentence to this effect in an article one day, but I can unfortunately no longer locate the source. I apologise if it was yours!

397 Alastair McIntosh, *Hell and High Water, Birlinn 2008:162*

398 David C. Korten, *When Corporations Rule the World*, Kumarian Press, Connecticut 2001